"Wiegartz and Gyoerkoe have written an invaluable guide for overc̶o̶m̶m̶a̶ ̶-̶ ̶t̶i̶o̶n̶ in the context of worry and anxiety. The book teaches readers to ̶ ̶ ̶ ̶ ̶ ̶ ̶ ̶ ̶ ̶ ̶ and provides them with effective, step-by-step strategies for dealing with procrastination and overcoming anxiety and perfectionism, which often contribute to procrastination. I highly recommend this book for anyone whose anxiety prevents them from getting things done. Don't put it off—read this book now!"

—Martin M. Antony, Ph.D., ABPP, professor in the department of psychology at Ryerson University and author of *When Perfect Isn't Good Enough* and *The Anti-Anxiety Workbook*

"Problems associated with chronic procrastination have been largely overlooked in self-help literature. Drawing upon the latest findings from clinical research, Pamela Wiegartz and Kevin Gyoerkoe provide practical tools to help people make timely decisions and stop putting important aspects of their life on hold."

—C. Alec Pollard, Ph.D., director of the Anxiety Disorders Center at Saint Louis Behavioral Medicine Institute and professor of family and community medicine at Saint Louis University

"In a straightforward and practical manner, Wiegartz and Gyoerkoe have provided a highly useful set of tools for helping readers overcome the widespread problem of procrastination. Not only do they address the basics of goal setting, motivation, and how to use established cognitive and behavioral methods, they also incorporate newer approaches, such as mindfulness, into this easy-to-read book."

—Cheryl Carmin, Ph.D., director of the stress and anxiety disorders clinic and the cognitive behavioral therapy program at the University of Illinois at Chicago

"Change your thinking; change your life! Seasoned clinicians Wiegartz and Gyoerkoe bring their extensive expertise from the consulting room into the pages of this clearly written self-help guide. They concisely explain the fundamental thought processes that lead to procrastination, teach the reader how to rationally examine and challenge those thoughts, and then gently but firmly move the reader forward from anxiety and self-doubt to a sense of efficacy and accomplishment!"

—Aaron Nelson, Ph.D., ABPP, chief of psychology and neuropsychology at Brigham and Women's Hospital and assistant professor at Harvard Medical School

"No matter what you procrastinate about, *The Worrier's Guide to Overcoming Procrastination* will help you gain insight into the habits that hold you back and provide you with real-world practices to overcome them. By learning and following the practices in this book, you'll be able to experience how wonderful it feels not to be a habitual procrastinator."

—David Haddad, president of Vidacom Corporation in Chicago, IL

The Worrier's Guide to Overcoming Procrastination

Breaking Free from the Anxiety that Holds You Back

Pamela S. Wiegartz, Ph.D.
Kevin L. Gyoerkoe, Psy.D.

New Harbinger Publications, Inc.

Distributed in Canada by Raincoast Books

Copyright © 2010 by Pamela S. Wiegartz and Kevin L. Gyoerkoe
New Harbinger Publications, Inc.
5674 Shattuck Avenue
Oakland, CA 94609
www.newharbinger.com

Acquired by Tesilya Hanauer; Cover design by Amy Shoup; Edited by Carole Honeychurch

FSC
Mixed Sources
Product group from well-managed
forests and other controlled sources
Cert no. SW-COC-002283
www.fsc.org
© 1996 Forest Stewardship Council

RAINFOREST ALLIANCE
CERTIFIED

Library of Congress Cataloging-in-Publication Data

Wiegartz, Pamela S.
  The worrier's guide to overcoming procrastination : breaking free from the anxiety that holds you back
/ Pamela S. Wiegartz and Kevin L. Gyoerkoe.
       p. cm.
  Includes bibliographical references.
  ISBN 978-1-57224-871-7 (pbk.) -- ISBN 978-1-57224-872-4 (pdf ebook) 1. Procrastination. 2. Anxiety.
3. Worry. I. Gyoerkoe, Kevin L. II. Title.
  BF637.P76W54 2010
  155.2'32--dc22
                                    2010043967

12 11 10   10 9 8 7 6 5 4 3 2 1   First printing

To Tommy and Jack—my favorite reasons to procrastinate

—PSW

For Kody

—KLG

Contents

Acknowledgments vii

Introduction 1

PART 1
Learn About Your Anxiety and Procrastination

1

Understanding Anxious Procrastination 7

2

Evaluate Your Reasons for Procrastinating. 15

3

Get Motivated and Make a Commitment 21

PART 2
Change Your Mind About Anxiety and Procrastination

4

Overcome Fears of Failure *and* Success 31

5

Know That You Can Do It. 51

6

Accept Imperfection and Uncertainty 63

7

Focus on the Now 73

PART 3

Get Moving on Your Goals

8

Confront Your Fears 87

9

Set Effective Goals 97

10

Manage Time More Effectively 109

11

Change the Way You Relate. 127

PART 4

Maintain Positive Change

12

Get Support 143

13

Prevent a Relapse 149

References 157

Acknowledgments

We'd like to thank our editors at New Harbinger Publications—Tesilya Hanauer, Jess Beebe, and Carole Honeychurch—for their support, enthusiasm, and insightful contributions to this book. And thanks to our proofreader, Gloria Sturzenacker, for her keen attention to detail. You've been a pleasure to work with.

Of course, we want to thank our patients for giving us the opportunity to join them on the journey to overcoming anxious procrastination. They've taught us much about strength, courage, and perseverance, and we are grateful.

Thanks also to our families for their endless patience and encouragement during the late nights and weekends we spent writing. As with most things in our lives, we couldn't have done it without you!

Introduction

If you've picked up this book, we're excited to offer you hope. We know how difficult it is to overcome procrastination. If you're like most of our patients, you've tried many things already but still feel stuck. It seems that no matter how hard you try, your productivity just isn't where it should be and you can't stop putting things off. You know the consequences of procrastination: missed deadlines, overdue bills, unhappy supervisors, poor grades, and feelings of guilt and inadequacy. What you may not know is that procrastination is often driven by *anxiety*.

Though often overlooked, much of the time anxiety is really the driving force behind avoidance. Fear of failure, discomfort with success, and perfectionism all serve to feed anxiety and foster procrastination. You might have noticed how this works: you see an e-mail from your boss in your in-box about a project you're behind on and you feel a quick rush of adrenaline. You make a fast decision: *I can't deal with it*, and you get up to go talk to a coworker instead. Or you sit down with your tax documents and feel a sense of dread. You think to yourself, *I'm going to owe a lot of money*, and you close the file and turn on the TV. In time, you fall into the habit of avoiding tasks when you feel anxious, instead of confronting and completing them. Procrastination becomes a way of life.

The good news is that procrastination is a habit you can change. You can remove the chains of anxious avoidance and reclaim your life. You can develop the skills that will allow you to do what needs to be done and enjoy your life too. Successfully conquering anxious procrastination means you get to work productively and play happily. You'll get things done, *and* the time you spend relaxing and pursuing activities you enjoy will be free of the guilt that plagued you before. You'll finally be able to truly relax and have fun knowing that nothing is hanging over your head.

This book contains the tools you need to beat anxious procrastination—you'll find everything you need on these pages. Our hope is that you'll use the strategies in this book to conquer the procrastination that holds you back and experience the increased joy, productivity, and self-esteem that comes from facing your fears—and winning.

HOW TO USE THIS BOOK

As you read through *The Worrier's Guide to Overcoming Procrastination,* you'll notice that it contains four parts. In part 1 you'll learn about the relationship between anxiety and procrastination. You'll also identify the reasons behind your procrastination. At the end of part 1, you'll make a commitment to change. In part 2 you'll work on changing the negative thinking patterns that fuel your anxiety and procrastination. You'll unearth the fears of failure (or success) that lurk beneath your avoidance, and you'll boost your confidence to complete tasks. As you challenge your perfectionistic beliefs, you'll work on accepting the uncertainty inherent in life. Part 3 includes strategies to change your behavior and get you moving toward your goals. We'll show you how to set effective goals that will help boost your productivity and guide you through managing your time more skillfully. And lastly, in Part 4 we'll describe some of the ways you can maintain the positive changes you've worked so hard to achieve. You'll learn the key role social support plays in sustaining your progress, as well as other techniques to prevent a relapse.

Here are a few additional suggestions to get the most out of this book:

♦ Be sure to complete all the self-help exercises in this book. Just as reading the latest fashion magazine won't improve your wardrobe, you won't beat anxious procrastination just by reading about it. Pick up your pen or pencil—just like we ask our clients to do—and get to work.

♦ Keep at it! Though these strategies are fast and effective, anxiety and procrastination are a tough team. It takes time and work to master these skills and overcome anxious procrastination—but it *will* be worth it.

♦ Get additional help if you need it. If you've worked hard on the exercises in this book and still don't feel you're making the progress you desire, you can use this book in conjunction with a cognitive-behavioral therapist experienced in helping people overcome anxiety and procrastination.

♦ Reward yourself! Let's face it—change is difficult, and you deserve something for all of your hard work. It may be a small treat or something larger. Either way, give yourself credit for working so hard to overcome your anxious procrastination.

FROM THE AUTHORS

Pamela S. Wiegartz, Ph.D.

Over the years I've seen countless clients come into therapy asking for help with their procrastination. They are bright, capable, hardworking people who just can't seem to get things done on time and can't seem to figure out why. Many times my clients are surprised to hear that anxiety might be behind their avoidance. They already know they feel anxious *after* they put things off, but they often don't realize that it is their anxiety that leads them to procrastinate in the first place. For these clients, overcoming fear of failure, perfectionism, or even fear of success has been the key to conquering their procrastination and returning to productivity—or experiencing it for the first time! By using the same strategies I teach my clients, techniques based on years of clinical experience and the latest research findings, you too can develop the skills you need to free yourself from the anxiety that holds you back, overcome your procrastination, and live your life to the fullest. Good luck!

Kevin L. Gyoerkoe, Psy.D.

As a psychologist, I specialize in the treatment of anxiety disorders, and every day I see the toll they take on the lives of individuals who suffer from them. Fortunately, I also get to see those same people recover, put their problems behind them, and find the joy in living. While numerous books exist on procrastination, there's no other book quite like this one. This book addresses the anxiety that keeps you from productivity and leads you to procrastinate. In this book you'll find everything you need to defeat the anxiety that stands in your way.

Thank you for bringing us along on your journey to conquer this problem. I wish you great success in your endeavor to defeat anxious procrastination and regain a sense of calm and control in your life. The ideas and exercises in this book will serve as your guide to overcoming procrastination. With hard work and effort, you can do it. The benefits—increased self-esteem, lower anxiety, more productivity—will be well worth your efforts.

PART 1

Learn About Your Anxiety and Procrastination

Understanding Anxious Procrastination

No one is immune to the lure of procrastination. In fact, by the time that first sentence was written, our plants had been watered, e-mail checked, and dreaded trips to the gym completed. *Everyone* procrastinates at times. We do it when we're overwhelmed, fearful of outcomes, unsure of our abilities, or sometimes when we'd frankly just rather be doing something else. Everyone puts off decisions or tasks sometimes, but for many, procrastination stems from profound anxiety, worry, and self-doubt. For anxious procrastinators, avoiding and putting off tasks and decisions can become a chronic, debilitating problem.

The term "anxious procrastination" may be a new one to you. In fact, many people do not immediately recognize anxiety as the source of their procrastination—although they certainly notice the anxiety that results from their delay. We use the term *anxious procrastinator* to describe anyone who puts off or avoids tasks or decisions due to their worry and anxiety. This is not the harmless, occasional choice to enjoy a beautiful spring day rather than clean out the garage. Anxious procrastination is rooted in fear and self-doubt and can rob you of your self-confidence, cause you to put off important decisions, and lead you down a path of escalating anxiety. If you are an anxious procrastinator, this behavior may prevent you from reaching your goals and recognizing your true potential.

This chapter is designed to give you an overview of what is known about the relationship between anxiety and procrastination. You'll learn about different types of procrastination, what factors contribute to delaying decisions or tasks, and the serious consequences procrastination can have. You'll also learn what you can do about it and how the techniques in this book can help.

WHAT IS PROCRASTINATION?

Many of us understand procrastination as intentionally putting off doing something that needs to be done. But this benign definition doesn't quite capture the drama involved for those who struggle with chronic procrastination. It also doesn't describe the relentless cycle of worry, guilt, and fear experienced by anxious procrastinators. *What if I can't do it? What if others find out about the "real" me? It's safer to not try than to fail. If it's not done right, what's the point of doing it at all?* These are the tenets of the anxious procrastinator. Sound familiar? If you struggle with procrastination, you already know how paralyzing this anxiety, fear, and self-doubt can be.

Behavioral Procrastination

Most people think of putting off activities like homework, chores, or paperwork when they hear the term procrastination. You may imagine someone watching TV or taking a nap to avoid working on a job that needs to be done. This type of delay—when you put off completing tasks—is called *behavioral procrastination* (McCown, Johnson, and Petzel 1989). When you don't mow your lawn or complete your taxes, you're engaging in behavioral procrastination.

Decisional Procrastination

There is another type of procrastination, though, that is often overlooked but is also associated with anxiety and worry (Spada, Hiou, and Nikcevic 2006). *Decisional procrastination* strikes when you shy away from decisions and put off choices to be made (Effert and Ferrari 1989). Agonizing over which microwave to buy or whether you paint your bedroom green or gray would be examples of decisional procrastination.

EXERCISE: Behavioral Procrastination or Decisional Procrastination?

See if you can identify each type in the following. Check one:

Vacuuming your floors instead of going to the gym

☐ Behavioral procrastination

☐ Decisional procrastination

Worrying about the consequences of choosing the wrong car

☐ Behavioral procrastination

☐ Decisional procrastination

Browsing the Internet to see if there are better topics for your paper

☐ Behavioral procrastination

☐   Decisional procrastination

Cleaning off your desk before you pay bills

☐   Behavioral procrastination

☐   Decisional procrastination

How did you do? Did you think that putting off going to the gym and paying bills were examples of behavioral procrastination? Good. If you also recognized that delaying your choice of car and paper topic illustrated decisional procrastination, you're right on track. Like most people, you may find that you struggle with both types of procrastination. That's okay, because the strategies you'll find in later chapters can be used to overcome both behavioral *and* decisional procrastination.

Now, can you think of times when you put off a task or a decision? Write them in the spaces below:

Behavioral Procrastination

Tasks I've recently put off:

_____

_____

_____

_____

_____

Decisional Procrastination

Decisions I've recently delayed:

_____

_____

_____

_____

_____

Don't worry if there weren't enough spaces to record all the tasks or decisions you've been avoiding—after all, you're just getting started on the path to beating procrastination. You'll use this list along with the exercises in chapter 2 to help you understand your reasons for procrastination and to begin crafting your individualized program.

HOW ANXIETY AND PROCRASTINATION INTERACT

To use the rest of this book effectively, it's important to understand how anxiety and worry lead to procrastination and the vicious cycle of delay and escalating anxiety. There is no shortage of research linking anxiety to procrastination (for instance, Fritzsche, Young, and Hickson 2003; Milgram and Toubiana 1999), and it appears that increased anxiety is associated with both decisional and behavioral types (Spada, Hiou, and Nikcevic 2006). In fact, factors associated with anxiety are not only linked to procrastination but often cited in the literature as its source (for example, Brownlow and Reasinger 2000; Senecal, Lavoie, and Koestner 1997).

Can you recall a time when you felt anxious about a task or decision and chose to put it off? What happened? Did your anxiety temporarily ease? How about as the deadline approached? Did anxiety rise or fall? If you're like most anxious procrastinators, delaying a dreaded task or choice initially leads to a brief respite from anxiety and worry. Maybe you can even convince yourself that whatever you're doing during this delay is more important than the original task. However, the anxiety never really disappears—you know you *should* be working on the task or decision—and as time passes and the deadline approaches, anxiety continues to grow. Fears of evaluation become magnified and doubts about the outcome loom as you wonder whether you'll have time to complete the task well enough (or at all), particularly now that so much time has been wasted. Guilt over procrastinating and paralyzing fears of failure combine to stymie your productivity. In the best scenario, the job gets done with no catastrophic consequences, but even so, you're exhausted, feeling terrible about yourself, and primed to start the whole process over again.

Sources of Anxiety

It's clear to most people that, once procrastination starts, it is a self-perpetuating process. But you may wonder, "Where does my initial anxiety come from? Why do I put things off in the first place?" This is an important question with a complicated answer. In fact, the answer will be different for each person reading this book. It seems that anxious procrastination results from the complex interplay between a number of variables, like self-doubt (Tan et al. 2008), fear of failure (Onwuegbuzie and Collins 2001), and perfectionism (Stöber and Joormann 2001). Here is an overview of the key players.

SELF-DOUBT

When you believe you have the capability to successfully complete tasks, wonderful things can happen. If you doubt your ability to do well, guess what? You're more likely to procrastinate (Tan et al. 2008; Steel 2007). Low *self-efficacy*, or the belief that you do not have the ability to accomplish a particular task, has been repeatedly linked to procrastination (Bandura 1997). For many anxious procrastinators, this self-doubt can be at the root of their delay behavior.

One of our clients, Jenni, was a bright and promising young graduate student. A year away from completing her doctorate in biology, she found herself seemingly further and further away from completing her dissertation. As deadlines came and went, Jenni found her anxiety skyrocketing. She was unable to explain to her professors why her dissertation work went undone, particularly after her coursework had gone so well. In our therapy sessions, Jenni revealed that, while she was confident in her ability to memorize and test well on material, she had immense self-doubt about her ability to produce quality, original work. She just didn't think she could do it. Because of her self-doubt, she avoided situations or tasks—like her dissertation—that required creativity and original thought.

If, like Jenni, you find that self-doubt is behind your anxiety and procrastination, the exercises in chapter 5 will be of particular value to you. Keep in mind that while Jenni's self-doubt lay in one specific area, low self-efficacy can strike across multiple domains. You'll learn more about your individual pattern of anxiety and procrastination in chapter 2.

FEAR OF FAILURE

Similarly, fear of failure has been long thought to be a culprit in procrastination, and research has confirmed the association (for instance, Onwuegbuzie and Collins 2001). Worrying that the outcome of our work may be negative is a stumbling block for many otherwise competent and promising people. In fact, promising individuals may be particularly susceptible to fears that they will fall short of expectations simply because the expectations are so high.

Calvin was a highly recruited job candidate out of college. He was charming, affable, and bright. When he took a marketing job at a well-respected international firm, everyone, including Calvin, had high hopes for his future. He liked his new boss and was excited about the prospect of excelling in this new environment. However, Calvin soon found himself shrinking from the attention his colleagues gave him and spending more and more time in his office alone. Fearful that he would offer an uninformed opinion or answer a question incorrectly, Calvin was often silent in meetings and quickly changed the subject with coworkers when the discussion turned toward topics unfamiliar to him. In the days preceding his first major presentation, he found himself paralyzed by the idea of sharing his thoughts with others. He focused on trivial details like finding the right size and color of the font on his slides and honing his opening line, rather than the substance of his talk. Or he'd avoid his anxiety altogether by sleeping or watching television. Calvin's fear that his boss might be disappointed in him was devastating. He stayed up the entire night before his presentation worrying that he would be revealed as an imposter and, in the morning, ended up calling in sick to avoid his fears.

Like Calvin and other anxious procrastinators, fear of failure may be the driving force behind your behavior. Fears of not living up to expectations or of disappointing yourself or others may keep you up at night imagining vivid failure scenarios. In some cases, procrastinating may actually serve as a mechanism to protect you from these fears. After all, if you'd put more time into your preparation, the result certainly would have been better, right? For some, failing by not putting forth full effort may be less threatening than doing your best and having it come up short. If you feel that fears of failure contribute to your procrastination, chapter 4 will help you break through this anxiety and move toward achieving your goals.

FEAR OF SUCCESS

Believe it or not, sometimes it's not fear of failure but fear of *success* that drives procrastination (Burka and Yuen 2008). Putting off tasks and failing on purpose can be a way of fending off the attention or higher expectations that come with success. Or procrastinating may serve as a form of self-sabotage in someone who doesn't believe she deserves to succeed. Sometimes delay and avoidance can result from discrepancies between a person's concept of success and how a person views himself or his environment.

John, for instance, was the youngest child of six in an immigrant family. They lived in a working-class neighborhood where a large proportion of the families were of the same ethnicity as John's family. His parents valued education and, while all of his siblings went on to college, John was clearly the most academically gifted of the bunch. With all of his brothers and sisters already away at college, John's success at school made him the target of neighborhood bullies who accused him of thinking he was "too good" for everyone. While John had always been proud of his accomplishments, without the support of his siblings, he slowly began to put off his homework in favor of hanging out with friends. He began putting off studying, waiting until the last minute to prepare for tests, if he studied at all. His grades began dropping, but John actually felt relieved. He felt that by being average, he fit in better and was more accepted by his peers.

The reasons for fear of success are many. It's up to you to figure out whether this worry underlies your procrastination and, if so, what those fears are for you. Chapter 4 will help you to examine your possible fear of success and help you to develop strategies to overcome it so you won't need procrastination anymore.

PERFECTIONISM

The relationship between procrastination and perfectionism is a complicated one, and the link between the two is not always clear cut (Steel 2007). Some researchers find worry, perfectionism, and procrastination to be associated (Stöber and Joormann 2001), while other studies have suggested that certain types of perfectionism may actually be of benefit (Klibert, Langhinrichsen-Rohling, and Saito 2005). In our experience, perfectionism and procrastination go hand in hand. We find that the higher and more unrealistic the standards, the greater the anxiety that accompanies the task. While it may be that some degree of perfectionism is a good thing, it doesn't take much to tip the scales to paralyzing anxiety and overwhelming goals. For a large subset of our clients who procrastinate, the effects of perfectionism are clearly detrimental.

Marla was a stay-at-home mom living in a nice suburb in the Midwest. With a two-year-old and a baby on the way, her friends and family attributed her inability to get things accomplished to the situation. But Marla had always struggled with perfectionism and procrastination. From finding the perfect wording for her high school essays to picking out the correct flowers for her wedding, every decision seemed monumental to her—the options endless and the "right" answer unclear. In the past, things had always gotten accomplished eventually, but, with the additional responsibilities of parenthood, Marla fell farther and farther behind. She had rigid rules about how things should be done, and those rules cost her hours and hours of lost time and very rarely resulted in the task being done or the decision made. The search for her toddler's first car seat meant hours online searching product reviews, safety websites, and discussion-board opinions. She created spreadsheets listing pros and cons for each seat and was overwhelmed by the amount of information and the number of conflicting views. No seat seemed to be good enough, safe enough, or the right color or to have the right options. Paralyzed by the need to find the perfect choice, she was unable to move forward. Marla finally relented, asking her husband to purchase the seat when the task absolutely couldn't be put off any longer. With high standards and sensitivity to possible mistakes, Marla's flower beds remain empty, her house unpainted, and the baby's room unfurnished.

As Marla's story illustrates, perfectionism can be a powerful deterrent to productive action. If the quest to avoid errors and find the perfect option is a familiar one to you, you will find chapter 6 helpful. There you'll learn more about how to counter perfectionistic beliefs, live with uncertainty, and tolerate the imperfection inherent in life—and procrastinate less as a result.

How These Anxieties Work Together

So now you know the factors that play a key role in anxious procrastination. And, as you may have noticed, they have a close relationship to one another. Fear of failure can lead to perfectionistic rumination, the way Calvin's anxiety about not measuring up at his job led to his focus on trivial aspects of his work. Perfectionism lends itself to self-doubt, as with Marla's doubt of her choices and quest for perfection. And self-doubt can certainly contribute to fear of failing, as with Jenni's doubts about her ability to create original work resulting in her worry that she'd fail at her dissertation. All of these variables and more interact with one another to result in anxious procrastination. They affect each person in a distinct way and in unique combinations, but the end result is the same—anxiety, worry, and avoidance that hobble productivity and prevent you from reaching your goals. Use the subsequent chapters to determine the role of these factors in your anxiety and procrastination and learn how to change them.

CAN PROCRASTINATION EVER BE A GOOD THING?

If you've picked up this book, the answer for you is probably no. The fact that you're looking for strategies to change your behavior likely means that procrastination is troublesome to you. Some investigators, however, argue that not all procrastination is bad (Chu and Choi 2005). They distinguish between two types of procrastinators: passive and active. Anxious procrastinators fall into the first category—they are paralyzed by worry and indecision and fail to complete tasks on time despite intending to do so. Active procrastinators, on the other hand, delay actions deliberately and instead focus attention on other important tasks. Perhaps they like to work under pressure or feel challenged by approaching deadlines. Active procrastinators look very different from passive procrastinators. They use time more purposefully, feel more in control of their time, are less avoidant, and have lower stress levels and higher self-efficacy (Chu and Choi 2005).

EXERCISE: Are You an Active Procrastinator or a Passive Procrastinator?

Take a look at the lists below and check off the items that best describe you.

Active Procrastinator	Passive Procrastinator
☐ Chooses to delay tasks	☐ Doubts ability as deadline approaches
☐ Completes tasks on time	☐ Has guilt over delaying behavior
☐ Enjoys the challenge of deadlines	☐ Gets stressed about deadlines
☐ Feels in control of time	☐ Uses avoidance to cope

If you identify more with the passive procrastinator, you probably don't need a book to tell you how procrastination interferes with your life. Anxious procrastinators are all too familiar with the missed opportunities, damaged relationships, and shame that go along with putting things off. Procrastination interferes with performance (Sub and Prabha 2003), leads to higher stress and poorer health (Sirois, Melia-Gordon and Pychyl 2003), and impairs financial and career success (Mehrabian 2000). But the good news is that, by picking up this book, you've taken the first step toward regaining control of your life, changing your behavior, and meeting your goals.

NEXT STEPS

In the chapters that follow you'll find tools to assess your individual patterns of procrastination, cognitive-therapy strategies to change the beliefs that lead to anxiety, and behavioral techniques to help you face your fears and manage your time more effectively. Although it may be tempting, don't skip over any chapters or exercises—there is no quick fix to procrastination, and this book is designed to help you both understand the reasons why you put things off and learn practical strategies for change. The book will benefit you most if you read the chapters in the order they are presented and complete each exercise for yourself. Now that you understand the factors that can lead to anxious procrastination, you're ready to get to work. Start now down the path to productivity, improved self-confidence, and fulfilled potential!

Key Points

- ◆ Everyone procrastinates at times, but for many it becomes chronic and problematic.

- ◆ The term "anxious procrastinator" refers to people who put off tasks or decisions due to anxiety and worry.

- ◆ Behavioral procrastination is the putting off of tasks, and decisional procrastination is the delaying of choices.

- ◆ In anxious procrastinators, self-doubt, fear of failure, and perfectionism interact to interfere with productivity.

- ◆ Procrastination can hinder performance and lead to higher stress, poorer health, and decreased financial and career success.

Evaluate Your Reasons for Procrastinating

Isabella faces a hard deadline. She has to finish a major presentation to her board, and it's due next week. She's stuck. She's trying to work, trying to finish the presentation on time, but she finds herself distracted by almost everything—cleaning, checking her e-mail, reorganizing her files. She's doing everything but working on her presentation. Each time she sits down to work, a wave of panic hits her and horrible images flood her mind. She imagines the projector not working, spilling her coffee, becoming tongue tied. Mostly, though, she pictures the members of the board ripping her to shreds. She imagines them seated at the boardroom table, the room darkened. They look stern, intimidating. She sees herself up in front of them, fumbling through her presentation, while they sit with arms crossed and shake their heads disapprovingly. And to top it all off, Isabella imagines at the end of her talk that the president of the board will simply say, "I'm sorry, Isabella. That wasn't good enough. You're fired."

Like Isabella, Jack has a deadline breathing down his neck. His boss asked him to submit a report on the safety practices of the plant he works in before they have their annual review. If Jack doesn't complete the report by the deadline, his boss could get fired. Despite this pressure, Jack procrastinates, finding any excuse he can to avoid working on his project. But, unlike Isabella, Jack isn't afraid of failure. Jack fears success. As he sits down to work on his project, Jack thinks of doing an outstanding job. He imagines his boss and everyone else at the plant being thrilled with his work. But that thought doesn't motivate him, it fills him with dread. Suppose his boss is impressed. That might mean a promotion. He might get a new job with new responsibilities. He'd be faced with more pressure, more demands. Jack isn't sure he wants a promotion. He's pretty happy in his current job. However, more money for his family would be difficult to turn down. It's a problem Jack would rather not face. So instead of working on his project, he avoids it.

Henry doesn't have a deadline. But he does have a lot of uncompleted tasks. On one weekend, for example, Henry planned to paint the wall in the bathroom, find a new dentist, and replace his old TV.

Unfortunately, Henry didn't complete any of these tasks. He was surprised when Sunday night rolled around. "Where did the weekend go?" he wondered. He promised himself he'd do it the next weekend. Soon, weekend after weekend passed and the tasks on Henry's list remained.

What stops Henry is perfectionism. He believes in the old adage "If you're going to do something, do it right." So he pours over paint colors, never quite finding the "right" one. He looks up dentists online and asks all his friends about their dentist, but he can't find one that meets his standards—each possibility seems to have a flaw. And he continues to research television sets, but can't bring himself to make a purchase.

Isabella, Jack, and Henry all have one thing in common. They are procrastinating, putting off or avoiding tasks that are important to them. However, they all have different reasons for procrastinating. Isabella fears failure, while Jack fears success. Henry's perfectionism stymies him. Like you, each has their own worries that lead to their procrastination. Understanding the underlying reasons behind your procrastination is a crucial step in overcoming anxious procrastination.

In this chapter, you'll learn to identify your key reasons for procrastination. First we will review common motivators for anxious procrastination, including fear of failure, fear of success, and perfectionism, and we'll introduce some others. Then you'll complete a brief self-assessment test. You'll check off which thought patterns apply to you, revealing which most often subvert your efforts. Then, armed with this information, you'll read about the next steps to take in overcoming anxiety, worry, and procrastination.

THE COMMON REASONS FOR ANXIOUS PROCRASTINATION

One of the most common questions we get as therapists is "Why do I procrastinate?" In our view, this question reflects the frustration that comes from suffering anxious procrastination. On the one hand, you know what you need to do. But you don't do it, or you wait until the last minute. And time and again the pattern repeats itself. You feel caught, trapped in a vortex of anxiety, worry, stress, and procrastination. We wrote this chapter to help you begin to answer the question "Why do I procrastinate?"

In Parts 2 and 3 of this book, you'll find effective strategies to help you overcome typical reasons for procrastination. Below, we'll briefly describe these reasons and then you'll complete a self-assessment test to see which most frequently lead to procrastination for you.

- **Fear of Failure**: The thought of putting in effort and still failing makes you anxious. Instead of trying and failing, you choose avoiding and procrastinating. You might especially fear the disapproval of others and feel that no matter what you do, you'll come up short.

- **Fear of Success**: The idea of doing well makes you nervous and panicky. You fear higher expectations, greater responsibilities, and undeserved accolades, and these fears lead you to procrastinate.

- **Low Self-Confidence**: You see yourself as incapable in general. You feel you aren't good enough and don't possess the traits that others have which allow them to do well.

◆ **Low Self-Efficacy**: You feel you're incapable of meeting the specific challenges of a task. You believe you lack the basic skills to get things done and often think, *This is too hard. I can't do it.*

◆ **Perfectionism**: You believe that things should be done perfectly. You might also believe that other people expect perfection from you. As a result, when faced with a task, you become overwhelmed and easily frustrated by your own unreasonable standards.

◆ **Difficulty with Uncertainty**: It's difficult for you to face the unknown, and you feel you must know the outcome before you start. However, since everything in life is uncertain to some extent, you get paralyzed by doubt and turn to worry and avoidance to deal with the uncertainty.

◆ **Difficulty Making Decisions**: You focus more on information gathering than on actually making a decision. This style of procrastination is closely tied to perfectionism, as you feel you must find out everything possible to avoid an error.

◆ **Task Aversion**: You tend to think about the unpleasantness of a task. Instead of focusing on the outcome or the pleasure of completing a task, you consider only the challenges of it. Once you've convinced yourself the task will be truly awful, you avoid it.

WHY DO YOU PROCRASTINATE?

The self-assessment test below will help you pin down the reasons why you procrastinate. We've listed the most common reasons underlying procrastination along with questions to help you assess your own tendencies. If your answer to a question is yes, put a check in the box.

Fear of Failure

☐ When faced with a task, do you think of all the ways it could go wrong?

☐ Do you imagine yourself failing instead of succeeding?

☐ Do you picture how important people in your life might react if you failed?

☐ Do you tend to blame your failures on things like lack of time or effort?

☐ Do you believe it's better to not try at all than to try your best and fail?

Fear of Success

☐ Do you fear change as a result of success?

☐ Are you overwhelmed by the possibility of new responsibilities or higher expectations if you are successful?

☐ Do you worry that success will alienate you from your friends or family?

☐ Do you feel success will ultimately lead to disappointing others or letting them down?

☐ Do you feel your success will lead to other people finding out about the "real you"?

Low Self-Confidence

☐ Do you see yourself as inadequate or inferior?

☐ Do you feel that you lack confidence?

☐ When other people ask you to do something, is your initial reaction "No" or "I can't"?

☐ Do you tend to defer to other people and let them complete tasks for you when possible?

☐ Is part of the reason you procrastinate that you don't see yourself as competent or capable?

Low Self-Efficacy

☐ When faced with a task, do you have a sense that you lack the ability to complete it?

☐ Do you feel that you lack the basic skills required to get a certain project done?

☐ Do you feel hopeless when faced with a challenging task?

☐ Do you find you give up too easily, feeling like you just can't do it?

☐ Do you feel that other people can do things better than you?

Perfectionism

☐ Do you believe that if you're going to do something, you should try to do it perfectly?

☐ Do you find it difficult to persist when things aren't going just right?

☐ Do you feel that others expect perfection from you?

☐ Would you rather avoid doing something than do it imperfectly?

☐ Do you find that when you do complete a task, it's overly time consuming and slow moving?

Difficulty with Uncertainty

☐ Do you find uncertainty uncomfortable?

☐ Do you feel you have to know the outcome of a project or task before you start?

☐ If you're faced with uncertainty, do you tend to worry and ruminate about it?

☐ Would you rather have a guaranteed bad outcome than be faced with uncertainty?

☐ Do you put off completing tasks if you don't know how they'll turn out?

Difficulty Making Decisions

☐ Do you seek out excessive amounts of information before making a decision?

☐ Does your belief that you have to make a perfect decision prevent you from making any decision?

☐ Do you focus more on not making a bad decision than getting things done?

☐ Do you feel paralyzed by your options when making a choice?

☐ Would you rather put off making a decision than make one you regret?

Task Aversion

☐ Do you express your resentment about a task by not doing it?

☐ Do you find it difficult to persevere if something is boring or unpleasant?

☐ Do you feel like you shouldn't have to do something if it's not enjoyable?

☐ Do you sometimes make a mountain out of a mole hill and convince yourself that a task will be horribly unpleasant before you even start it?

☐ Do you find that when you do complete a task, it usually isn't as bad as you thought it would be?

What Are Your Reasons for Procrastination?

The self-assessment test highlights the most common reasons for procrastination. Take a moment to look closely at your answers. If you're like most people, you checked questions from more than one area. For example, you might've checked off some items under Difficulty with Uncertainty, Low Self-Efficacy, and Fear of Success. Or you might've checked off items for both Fear of Success *and* Fear of Failure. It's typical to check off items in more than one category. The goal here is for you to start to pin down some of the most common reasons behind your procrastination.

Take another look at the categories on the checklist. Which areas have the most checked answers? Write them down:

The top three reasons underlying procrastination for me are:

1. _____

2. _____

3. _____

Consider the three areas that you listed. These are good places to focus your efforts as you work through this book. We strongly suggest reading the entire book, as this effort will allow you to arm yourself with all the tools you'll need to overcome your anxiety and procrastination. However, if there are particular fears or worries that you struggle with most, the table below will direct you to the chapters that specifically target those areas.

Where to Find Help

Fear of failure	Chapter 4
Fear of success	Chapter 4
Low self-confidence	Chapter 5
Low self-efficacy	Chapter 5
Perfectionism	Chapter 6
Difficulty with uncertainty	Chapter 6
Difficulty making decisions	Chapters 6, 8
Task aversion	Chapters 9, 11

NEXT STEPS

You've now learned the most common reasons people procrastinate, and you've identified your own personal reasons for procrastination. You've also identified which areas impact you the most. Now you're armed with crucial information to manage your procrastination. You'll use this information in the pages ahead to help you best utilize the strategies presented in this book.

Key Points

- There are common patterns of anxious procrastination: fear of failure, fear of success, low self-confidence, low self-efficacy, perfectionism, difficulty with uncertainty, difficulty making decisions, and task aversion.

- Identifying your typical reasons for procrastination is a key step in regaining control of your time.

- Once you've identified some of the reasons why you procrastinate, you can apply the techniques described in this book to overcome your procrastination.

Get Motivated and Make a Commitment

One of the keys to overcoming anxious procrastination is committing to change. However, often when we're considering making important personal changes in our lives, we feel a sense of ambivalence. You may feel the same about overcoming anxious procrastination. Part of you wants to change, and another part isn't so sure. Because overcoming anxious procrastination is a difficult task, you'll need strong motivation and a firm commitment to make this change in your life.

In this chapter, you'll find several worksheets designed to help you solidify your desire to change. First, you'll look at the costs and benefits of procrastination. Then you'll pinpoint key ways procrastination has caused problems in your life and you'll identify the benefits of beating procrastination. And at the end of the chapter, we'll ask you to make a public commitment to change.

THE NUTS AND BOLTS OF SUCCESS

If you're like most people, this isn't the first time you've tried to make changes in your life. Most of us try to change ourselves in some way at some point or another. Whether it's losing weight, exercising more, spending more time with our children, spending less money, quitting smoking, or something else, trying to make positive changes is a part of life.

Unfortunately, if you've tried to make changes in your life, you also know how difficult it is. Let's face it: changing is hard. We need look no further than our new year's resolutions for proof. Each year we start anew with a list of goals and plans. Yet, in most cases, these resolutions quickly fall by the wayside as we fall prey to our old habits.

As grim as that sounds, there are clear keys to success. As we mentioned at the beginning of this chapter, your success in overcoming anxious procrastination hinges largely on two key factors: motivation and commitment.

Motivation means you've decided that making changes is in your best interest. We know that motivation plays a central role in making changes. But what does it mean to be motivated? Experts in the study of motivation suggest that those who are highly motivated to make changes in their lives show three characteristics: they have decided that change is highly important to them, they feel confident in their ability to change, and they feel ready—that now is the time to change (Miller and Rollnick 2002). As you work through the exercises in this chapter, keep these three factors in mind.

Commitment—the other key factor in success—means you are willing to work consistently over time to achieve your goals. Making challenging personal changes means ups and downs. You'll find as you work on overcoming anxious procrastination that change is a bit of a roller coaster. You'll have moments of great progress and success. Then you'll have times of defeat and failure. During those moments, you might feel like a failure—that you just want to give up because you'll never succeed. It's your commitment that will see you through these tough times. It's your commitment that will give you the strength to work persistently to achieve your goals. The methods we describe in this book do work, but they will require your consistent effort over time to see results.

In the next sections, you'll work on building your motivation and solidifying your commitment to overcoming anxious procrastination.

Get Motivated

One of the main barriers to building motivation is that anxious procrastination actually has a number of benefits. Most people don't think of procrastination in these terms, that there are a lot of *good* things about it. We typically just think of procrastination as a negative thing. Since you're reading this book, chances are that you feel the same way.

However, there are real benefits to procrastination. The benefits of anxious procrastination are often hidden, but they can sap your motivation to change nonetheless. Some examples of the benefits of procrastination include:

◆ You get to put off unpleasant tasks in favor of more enjoyable things.

◆ Problems may end up getting solved without any effort from you.

◆ You can avoid the possibility of failure—or success.

◆ You get to avoid the discomfort of doing something you dread.

◆ You can avoid the anxiety you feel about the task.

◆ Someone may come to your rescue and do it for you.

◆ The demands placed on you get lifted because you dragged your feet.

Whatever the benefits of procrastination are for you, it can help to be aware of them as you work to turn your procrastination habits around.

Of course, procrastination also has its drawbacks. But as you compare the benefits and the drawbacks, which side wins out? Are there more costs or more benefits to your procrastination? To build true motivation to change, motivation that will see you through the hard work necessary to achieve your goals, it can be helpful to conduct a cost-benefit analysis to see if the costs of anxious procrastination do, in fact, outweigh the benefits.

EXERCISE: Do a Cost-Benefit Analysis

Using the worksheet that follows, you can take stock of your procrastination habit. You'll see that this sheet is divided down the middle. On the left side, under "Costs," you can list all the drawbacks of avoiding unpleasant tasks. On the right side, under "Benefits," list all the benefits of putting off tasks. We've listed five spaces. However, you may find you need more for your list. Please feel free to add more if needed.

Cost-Benefit Analysis

Costs

1. _____

2. _____

3. _____

4. _____

5. _____

Benefits

1. _____

2. _____

3. _____

4. _____

5. _____

Sheila filled out her cost-benefit analysis like this:

Cost-Benefit Analysis

Costs

1. *I'm falling behind at work.*

2. *I feel lousy about myself.*

3. *I received a poor evaluation.*

4. *Friends and family are frustrated with me.*

5. *I'm performing below my capabilities.*

Benefits

1. *I do other things that are more fun.*

2. *I don't have to face my fears of failure.*

3. *I feel my time is my own.*

4. *I don't have to put in much effort.*

5. *I can avoid the pressure of success.*

Now that you've listed all the costs and benefits of procrastination, take a close look at each side. Which wins? Is your procrastination mostly working for you or against you?

Get Ready

Now that you've taken stock of the costs and benefits of procrastination, let's assume you've decided that your procrastination is working more against you than for you. The next step is to determine if you're truly ready for change. By "ready," we mean that you've decided *now* is the right time to work on overcoming your procrastination—that you've determined that you're motivated to make a change and ready to do so now.

To get ready, you'll need to take two steps: identify the benefits of overcoming procrastination and set a realistic and productive goal.

THE BENEFITS OF BEATING PROCRASTINATION

Now take the time to look into the future and see how all your hard work will pay off. Just as one might start an exercise program with an eye toward a long-term goal of losing weight, lowering cholesterol, and leading a longer, higher-quality life, you can peer into your crystal ball and envision how your life might improve if you conquered your anxious procrastination. Take a moment and consider all the benefits to defeating procrastination. List these benefits in the worksheet below:

The Benefits of Overcoming Procrastination

1. _____

2. _____

3. _____

4. _____

5. _____

6. _____

7. _____

8. _____

9. _____

10. _____

Jonathan's sheet looked like this:

The Benefits of Overcoming Procrastination

1. *I'll be more productive at work.*

2. *I'm more likely to get a raise.*

3. *I'll tackle small problems before they become bigger ones.*

4. *I'll feel better about myself, seeing myself as a more capable person.*

5. *I can stop beating myself up for procrastinating.*

6. *I'll master a valuable life skill—completing unpleasant tasks.*

7. *Other people will respect me more, seeing me as a leader.*

8. *I'll reap the benefits of my hard work and effort.*

9. *I'll avoid the consequences that come with procrastination.*

10. *I'll face my fears and learn to master them.*

SETTING GOALS

Even though this book is written to help you overcome anxious procrastination, everyone who reads it will have slightly different goals in mind. Perhaps you'd like to be more productive at work. Maybe you are a student and would like to stop pulling all-nighters. Or you might be in charge of running your household, and you'd like to stay ahead of the curve and not leave tasks undone or until the last minute. People who struggle with procrastination often have difficulty setting effective goals. In chapter 9, you'll learn step by step how to set goals that work for you. For now, however, we want you to think more generally about what you'd like to accomplish by reading this book. You can do it by completing this sentence: "After reading this book and working on the exercises in it, I will know I've made important changes in my life because I…

_____

_____

_____

FINAL CHECKLIST

Following is a checklist that covers the primary points from this chapter. To help you boost your motivation and commitment to changing your anxious procrastination, go ahead and consider each statement. Check yes or no as it applies to you.

	Yes	No
◆ My procrastination works more against me than for me.	_____	_____
◆ I see clear benefits from learning to defeat procrastination.	_____	_____
◆ Procrastination has had a detrimental effect on my life.	_____	_____
◆ I'm willing to work hard and apply the techniques in this book to decrease my anxious procrastination.	_____	_____
◆ I realize that conquering procrastination takes hard work and includes up and downs and setbacks.	_____	_____

If you answered yes to all of the above questions, you can move on to the next step. If you answered no to any, review that step and reevaluate. For example, are there benefits to overcoming procrastination that you've missed? Has procrastination cost you more than you think? Are you willing to put in the effort and cope with setbacks?

GO!

At this point, you've reviewed the costs and benefits of procrastination. You've discovered that procrastination actually has some powerful rewards, and you've brought those rewards to light and examined them to see if they are really worth the costs of procrastination. You also looked at the benefits of overcoming procrastination and set a clear, realistic, general goal for yourself.

Assuming you've decided that now is a good time to overcome procrastination and you are willing to work hard, it's time to take the final step in building your motivation: making a formal commitment to change.

EXERCISE: Make a Commitment—and Make It Public

Now that you've decided to work hard to conquer your procrastination, make a commitment to do so. Sign the following contract. Share it with someone close to you, a loved one or a good friend. Explain to them what you're doing and what you're trying to accomplish. Have this person sign as a witness.

The Anti-procrastination Contract

I am making a commitment to work hard on my anxious procrastination. I understand that time and effort are required to reach this goal, and I agree to work consistently over time to overcome this issue. I also understand that change is difficult and that I may feel frustrated at times and even have setbacks. However, after carefully reviewing the impact of procrastination on my life and the benefits of change, I am committing to taking control of my time and reducing the damaging effects of procrastination on my life.

Signed: _____ Date: _____

Witness: _____ Date: _____

NEXT STEPS

Now that you understand the factors that make up motivation and you've made a strong commitment to overcoming anxious procrastination, you're ready for the rest of this book. In the pages ahead, you'll find all the tools you need to decrease your anxiety, change your behavior, and overcome procrastination.

Key Points

♦ Remember that your success in overcoming procrastination depends largely on two keys: your motivation and your commitment to working hard to solve this problem.

♦ You can build your motivation by conducting a cost-benefit analysis. This will help you see the true costs of procrastination as well as exposing some of the hidden benefits of this habit.

♦ You can make sure you are ready to change by identifying the benefits of beating anxious procrastination and setting a clear, manageable goal.

♦ Once you've completed those steps, finalize your commitment by signing the Anti-Procrastination Contract and sharing your commitment with an important person in your life.

PART 2

Change Your Mind About Anxiety and Procrastination

4

Overcome Fears of Failure *and* Success

What if I fall short? I can't live up to these expectations. What if they're disappointed? What if they see the "real" me? And what if the "real" me isn't good enough? These thoughts spun through Maggie's head every Sunday night in anticipation of starting a new work week. She lay awake for hours picturing all the things that could go wrong that week and all the ways she would disappoint others: she wouldn't be prepared enough, she'd botch a project, embarrass her boss at a meeting, or overlook a key piece of research. The possibilities were endless and all equally terrifying to her.

If you are like many anxious procrastinators, fears of failure may keep you up at night imagining vivid scenarios of defeat. These fears can become paralyzing, making it difficult to get anything accomplished. Procrastination and avoidance may even keep you from reaching your goals altogether so that, ultimately, your fear of failure becomes a self-fulfilling prophecy.

Wayne lay awake and anxious on Sunday nights as well, but his thoughts sounded a bit different: *What if my boss gives me that promotion? I won't be able to handle the extra responsibility. My friends at work won't want to hang out with me anymore if I'm "the boss." I don't like being in the spotlight. What if they find out I'm really not as good as they think?* Like Maggie, Wayne could vividly imagine his worst-case scenarios. He could see himself stressed and harried, his friends snubbing him in the lunch room, and the disappointment on his boss's face.

Wayne's thoughts show us that anxious procrastination can be rooted in fears of success as well. Just as debilitating as fear of failure, anxiety about succeeding can prevent you from completing tasks and ruin your productivity. This fear can even lead you to sabotage yourself and intentionally fail, just to avoid your fears. In this chapter you'll learn more about fear of failure and success, how your fearful thoughts and worry lead to anxiety and procrastination, and what to do about it.

FEAR OF FAILURE

Maybe Maggie's fears sound familiar to you. Isn't everyone anxious about the idea of failing? After all, it's rare in our society to find someone who *really* doesn't care whether they win or lose. It's about the journey and what you learn along the way? Your best is good enough? That level of enlightenment is usually reserved for Buddhist monks and sensitive Little League coaches. Nearly everyone fears failing to some degree or at one time or another. But it's when you equate successful performance with your worth as a person that serious anxiety and procrastination result.

Viewing achievement as the basis of our self-worth is a common pitfall. We are bombarded with messages of how wealth, beauty, and intelligence lead to contentment and happiness. Television and movies show powerful, brilliant, impeccably groomed men and women succeeding effortlessly and leading glamorous lives. It's sometimes easy to forget that these are fictional characters who have scripts that hand them witty lines and tell them what moves to make. Achievement in real life is much more like a roller-coaster ride full of starts and stops, ups and downs, successes and failures. Any one misstep or shortcoming doesn't define your entire self. The truth is that humans are complex creatures with strengths and weaknesses, and none of us can be reduced to simply a success or a failure.

Until now, procrastination may have been your strategy of choice for dealing with fear of failure without you even realizing it. Procrastination provides a buffer between performance and ability. If you didn't try your best, then the outcome doesn't *really* reflect your true potential. Of course you would have succeeded if you had put more effort into it, right? Procrastination becomes a handy scapegoat and insulates the anxious procrastinator from his fear. Avoidance protects you by never testing your true potential—failing due to procrastination is much less threatening than doing your best and having it come up short. Later in this chapter, you'll learn more helpful strategies to identify and counter the beliefs that contribute to your fears of failure and get in the way of your productivity. Then you won't need procrastination anymore.

FEAR OF SUCCESS

Perhaps you identified with Wayne and the idea of doing well makes you nervous. Unlike fear of failure, many anxious procrastinators aren't even aware that a fear of success drives their behavior. They just find themselves dragging their feet when the future is looking too bright, downplaying accomplishments, or maybe allowing someone else to take credit for their work. If Wayne's thoughts rang true to you, perhaps you dread the higher expectations and greater responsibilities associated with doing well. Or the idea of getting negative (or positive) reactions from others could make you cringe. Or maybe you just feel that you don't deserve success. Any of these or other possibilities could be behind your fear of success and resultant procrastination.

The most obvious reason to fear success is the increased pressure and attention that come with it. If you do well once, people will expect you to do well again. Maybe you don't want the increased stress that goes along with that responsibility. Or you may worry that you can't live up to that expectation. What if you just got lucky this time? For some anxious procrastinators, it feels like you don't need to fail to let others down—even succeeding is a way to eventually disappoint.

Or maybe, like Wayne, you think that succeeding may distance you from friends or family. *People won't like me if I'm too successful. They'll see me as arrogant or competitive. My victory is someone else's loss.* These fallacies drive fear of success for some anxious procrastinators and lead them to sabotage themselves by doing poorly or putting off tasks. To keep balance and harmony, they try to fit into the crowd. Success becomes an embarrassment, and distinguishing oneself is seen as selfish, greedy, or competitive. Failing by "choice" through procrastination is viewed as preferable to the consequences of losing friendships or being seen as an outsider.

Some anxious procrastinators don't think they are worthy of success. It just doesn't fit in with their self-image. For them, the idea of succeeding just feels foreign, and they can't imagine themselves in that role. If this is the case for you, chapter 5 will help you to work through any self-esteem or confidence issues that lead you to procrastinate.

In many ways, fear of success and fear of failure are quite similar. Both may result from underlying insecurity and self-doubt, both cause intense anxiety, both result in procrastination as a coping strategy, and both hold you back from realizing your true potential.

YOUR THOUGHTS AND ANXIETY

To begin to tackle procrastination, you need to first recognize the important role your fears play in putting things off. Your fearful thoughts have a powerful impact on how you feel and, subsequently, on your behavior. For example, you might've noticed that, like Maggie or Wayne, when you're feeling anxious your mind is filled with negative, frightening thoughts and images. To cope, you avoid by putting off tasks or decisions and focusing your attention on other things. This connection between your thoughts, how you feel, and what you do is the basis for a type of treatment known as *cognitive behavioral therapy* (CBT). Cognitive behavioral therapy is based on the simple yet powerful idea that your thoughts impact your moods and that by changing your thinking, you can change how you feel (Beck et al. 1979). Decades of research have shown that cognitive behavioral therapy is a highly effective way to alleviate anxiety. You'll use CBT strategies in this chapter to help you pinpoint, evaluate, and counter the thoughts that contribute to your fear of failure, cause you anxiety, and lead you to procrastinate.

EXERCISE: Picture a Lemon

You can conduct your own experiment to test the impact of your thoughts on your feelings and behavior by completing the following exercise: Close your eyes and imagine a bright yellow lemon sliced in half on a clean, white plate. You see the juice from the lemon running onto the plate, and you smell the fresh, citrus scent. Now imagine that you pick up half of the lemon, squeeze it gently, and then take a bite into it. You taste the lemon juice and feel it on your tongue as your taste buds react to the sour flavor. Now, notice what's happening to you physically. Are you producing saliva? This is your body reacting to a vivid mental image—a thought. In fact, in many cases your body reacts as if what you imagine is actually happening.

As you can see from this exercise, your thoughts powerfully impact how you feel. And, just as your thoughts made your mouth water without food, they can also make you feel very stressed and anxious when there is no need to be. In other words, when you imagine a catastrophe, like blowing an exam, botching a work presentation, or disappointing someone you respect, you feel anxious. These thoughts and images make your muscles clench, your heart race, and your palms sweat, and they can lead you to avoid or procrastinate. If, up until now, procrastination has been your coping strategy of choice, that's understandable—it does work to some degree. Delaying a dreaded task or choice may give you temporary relief from your anxiety. Sometimes inaction even allows problems to just solve themselves. You know, however, that the task or issue usually remains, and as time passes and deadlines near, your anxiety just grows.

GETTING STARTED

In this chapter, you'll learn better strategies for dealing with your fearful thoughts and anxiety, tools that will allow you to return to productivity or perhaps experience it for the first time. There are five key steps to turning your fear of failure or success around and taking control of your anxious procrastination. These steps are:

1. Identifying your anxious thoughts

2. Labeling any distortions in your thinking

3. Replacing distorted thoughts with more accurate, realistic thinking

4. Examining the root of your fears

5. Getting practice confronting what you fear

Step One: Identify Your Fears

Before you learn to counter the fears that lead to your procrastination, you must identify the negative thoughts you have when you're feeling upset or anxious. Perhaps it's thoughts of screwing up a project at work, maybe you worry about making the wrong decision in your personal life, or it could be the images of the pressure and responsibility that come from success. This is your chance to learn what your own, individual anxious thoughts are and how they lead to avoidance and procrastination.

Think back over the past week and pick one situation that caused you to feel anxious. It could be at work, at school, at home, or anywhere. Now ask yourself what you were thinking at the time. What was going through your mind? What kind of thoughts do you recall? How about images?

Make copies of the chart on the next page so you can use it more than once. Then use the chart to briefly describe the situation that triggered your negative thinking. Note how you felt, then jot down your negative thoughts. For now, ignore the other three columns.

Thought Sheet

Situation	Feelings	Anxious Thoughts	Cognitive Distortions	Techniques	Rational Coping Responses

If, for any reason, you have trouble thinking of a situation of your own, you can use the exercise below to help you generate thoughts.

EXERCISE: Imagine Failure or Success

Pick one of the examples from this or previous chapters that illustrate fear of failure or success. Choose the one that you identify with most. Now close your eyes and picture yourself in the position of Calvin or John (from chapter 1) or Isabella or Jack (from chapter 2). Try to really imagine that you are in their shoes. How do you feel? What thoughts are going through your mind? Record those thoughts on the thought sheet.

For example, take a look at Maggie's thought sheet. Maggie is a production assistant at a local radio station. Her boss is rather demanding, and Maggie is often called upon to come up with innovative ideas or carry out complicated requests. Maggie is afraid of her boss and dreads going to work each day, fearing that this is the day "the other shoe will drop."

Maggie's Thought Sheet: Step One

Situation	Feelings	Anxious Thoughts
At our monthly meeting, my station manager reveals pending budget cuts and tells us that she'll be meeting with each of us individually to discuss our ideas for improving the station. She also scheduled weekly brainstorming meetings with the whole staff.	*Anxious*	*I won't be able to think of anything useful.* *I should be coming up with better ideas.* *If we all spend more time together, everyone will see that I'm not really competent.* *What if I get fired? I'll be devastated.* *Maybe being fired would be better than having everyone at work thinking I'm a loser.*

As you can see, hearing that expectations were being ramped up and more teamwork would be required triggered Maggie's fear of failure. The thoughts Maggie recorded center on her perceived incompetence and fears of falling short and disappointing others. She even wonders whether being fired might be better than failing. Can you see how this thought might lead to avoidance or procrastination behavior?

EXERCISE: Record Your Thoughts

For the next week, whenever you feel anxious or find yourself procrastinating, keep track of your thoughts using a thought sheet. Note the situation, the feelings you experience, and the thoughts you have. Be specific. Try to note exactly what is going through your mind (or what you were thinking and feeling at the time, if the incident happened in the past).

Step Two: Label Any Distortions in Your Thinking

Now that you've identified the thoughts that make you feel anxious, let's take a closer look at them. When you're feeling anxious or upset, your thoughts are often *distorted*. To say a thought is distorted means that it is unrealistic or illogical in some way.

Below, we've listed some of the most common ways thinking can get distorted, along with some examples for each type of distortion. Take a look at this list and consider your own thoughts. Do any of these distortions sound familiar?

All-or-nothing thinking. *All-or-nothing thinking*, or black-and-white thinking, means seeing the world in extreme categories. For example, you might describe your work as "great" or "horrible," "perfect" or "rotten." By viewing the world in this way, you ignore the shades of gray, the subtleties of life, and you force experiences into either-or categories. Examples of all-or-nothing thinking include:

◆ *I totally bombed that presentation.*

◆ *I am completely irresponsible.*

◆ *That mistake ruined everything.*

Overgeneralization. When you're engaged in the cognitive distortion of *overgeneralizing*, it means you're making global inferences based on a few experiences. You might also call this "painting with a broad brush." One clue that you're overgeneralizing is the presence of the words "always" or "never" in your thoughts. Here are a few examples of overgeneralizing:

◆ *I always screw things up.*

◆ *I'm never on time.*

◆ *My whole life is a mess.*

Fortune telling. With anxious procrastination, it's as if you've already failed before you even start. When you distort your thoughts with *fortune telling*, you overlook how hard it is to accurately predict the future, and you make what feel like iron-clad guarantees about what will happen next. Here are some examples of fortune telling:

- *This meeting will be useless.*

- *I'll probably get fired.*

- *I'll never get it together.*

Mind reading. As you might guess, *mind reading* happens a lot with fear of failure or success. Like the name suggests, mind reading means guessing what others are thinking—mostly speculating that they're thinking negatively about you. Usually there is little or no evidence to support this assumption. Below we've listed some examples of mind reading:

- *My coworkers are jealous of me.*

- *Everyone knows how inept I am.*

- *They see through me.*

Catastrophic thinking. When you're engaged in *catastrophic thinking*, you take minor setbacks and view them as horrible, awful, and unbearable. In fact, those are key words to watch out for when you're on the lookout for catastrophic thinking. If you notice words such as "awful," "horrible," or "terrible" crossing your mind in reaction to minor difficulties, chances are you're engaged in catastrophic thinking. Examples of catastrophic thinking include:

- *If I lost my job, my life would be over.*

- *It would be awful if others noticed my hands shaking.*

- *If I choose the wrong one, I'll regret it forever.*

Should statements. *Should statements* are rigid rules about how you and the world "should" be. They make you feel pressured, rushed, and stressed. If you direct a should toward yourself, you'll feel guilty and inadequate. Shoulds are impossible to live up to, so they often make you feel like a failure. Examples of should statements include:

- *I should keep a perfectly clean house.*

- *I should get straight A's.*

- *I should always know the right answer.*

Discounting the positives. If you fear failure, it's often hard to acknowledge the positive things you do. If you fear success, it's hard to imagine what could be positive about succeeding. If you *discount the* *positives*, you insist that the good things you do don't count and instead dwell exclusively on the negatives in yourself or the situation. Here are a few examples of discounting the positives:

◆ *I don't deserve credit for that—it was just luck.*

◆ *It doesn't matter if my idea was good, the typos killed it.*

◆ *So what if my boss liked what I did? It just made my coworkers look bad.*

"What if?" thinking. *"What if?" thinking* means you scare yourself with thoughts about bad things happening in the future. "What if?" thinking is one of the most common distortions in anxious procrastinators. If you fear failure or success, this distortion is likely one of the culprits. Examples of this kind of distortion include:

◆ *What if I forget my lines?*

◆ *What if I miss an important piece of research?*

◆ *What if I can't handle the pressure?*

Mental filtering. *Mental filtering* means picking a negative aspect of a situation and dwelling on it. In reality, every performance is a complex mix of both positives and negatives. Ruminating only on the negatives increases your anxiety and ruins any enjoyment or sense of accomplishment you might get. Here are a few examples of mental filtering:

◆ *I can't believe I mispronounced that word.*

◆ *He was texting during my pitch; I must have been really boring.*

◆ *That stain on my blouse made me look totally unprofessional.*

Discounting your coping skills. *Discounting your coping skills* means that you're telling yourself that you can't cope with difficulties, challenges, or setbacks. Saying you can't deal with failing or that you couldn't live up to the demands of success are common ways people discount their ability to cope. Some examples of these thoughts are:

◆ *I couldn't take it.*

◆ *I can't stand it.*

◆ *I don't handle challenges well.*

Now that you're familiar with the different types of cognitive distortions, let's see if you can find any distortions in your negative thoughts. Choose a thought from your thought sheet and take a look at the list of cognitive distortions. What distortions do you see in your thought? Keep in mind that one thought can contain many different distortions.

For example, let's take a look at the thoughts Maggie recorded on her thought sheet.

Maggie's Thought Sheet: Step Two

Situation	Feelings	Anxious Thoughts	Cognitive Distortions
At our monthly meeting, my station manager reveals pending budget cuts and tells us that she'll be meeting with each of us individually to discuss our ideas for improving the station. She also scheduled weekly brainstorming meetings with the whole staff.	Anxious	I won't be able to think of anything useful.	Fortune telling, All-or-nothing thinking
		I should be coming up with better ideas.	Should statement, Discounting the positives
		If we all spend more time together, everyone will see that I'm not really competent.	Mind reading, All-or-nothing thinking
		What if I get fired? I'll be devastated.	"What-if?" thinking, Catastrophic thinking, Discounting coping skills
		Maybe being fired would be better than having everyone at work thinking Im a loser.	Mindreading, Discounting coping skills

You can see from Maggie's sheet that each of her thoughts contained more than one distortion and that her "favorites" were mind reading, all-or-nothing thinking, and discounting coping skills.

Following is a shorthand list of the common cognitive distortions. You'll be using it as a checklist in a moment.

Cognitive Distortions

☐ 1. **All-or-Nothing Thinking:** You force experiences into extreme, black-or-white categories. You see things in just two categories, such as good/bad or perfect/failure.

☐ 2. **Overgeneralization:** You make broad, global inferences based on just a few events. Tip-offs include the presence of "always" or "never."

☐ 3. **Fortune Telling:** You make iron-clad predictions about dire things happening in the future.

☐ 4. **Mind Reading:** Without evidence, you imagine that you know what others are thinking about you—usually guessing that it's negative.

☐   5.   **Catastrophic Thinking:** You take a minor setback and view it as horrible, awful, or terrible.

☐   6.   **Should Statements:** You apply rigid, absolute rules to yourself and others about how things should and shouldn't be.

☐   7.   **Discounting the Positives**: You insist that the good things you or others do don't count.

☐   8.   **"What If?" Thinking:** You think "What if?" thoughts about bad things happening in the future.

☐   9.   **Mental Filtering:** You focus on one or a few negative aspects of a situation and allow that focus to spoil the whole thing.

☐   10.   **Discounting Your Coping Skills:** You tell yourself that you can't cope with problems or difficulties.

Look at the other thoughts on your thought sheet. Using the list of cognitive distortions, see what distortions you can find in your thoughts.

Do this exercise as many times as you like until you feel comfortable recognizing the cognitive distortions in your thoughts. Put a checkmark next to the distortions on the list that seem to pop up frequently for you. Pay special attention to those as you continue to work on changing your fearful thoughts.

Step Three: Change Your Thoughts

Now that you've learned to identify the fearful thoughts that reflect your fear of failure or success and know the common ways that your thoughts can get distorted, it's time to learn some methods to turn your thinking around. The techniques listed below are key strategies for thinking in a more balanced way and examining your fears realistically.

Examine the evidence. When we have negative thoughts, we often accept them as gospel without critically examining them. We assume that our fearful evaluation is correct and don't even stop to question it. One way to challenge your negative thoughts is to closely examine the evidence for and against them. You can do this by asking yourself the following questions about your negative thoughts:

◆   What's the evidence in favor of my negative thought?

◆   What's the evidence against my negative thought?

◆   Which side is more convincing?

◆   What should I do now?

Generate alternatives. When you feel anxious, you mentally lock in on the worst-case scenario. For example, if a coworker smiles at you, you might think, "He knows I'm not prepared." Or if your friend is quiet and withdrawn one day, you tell yourself, "She's put off by my know-it-all-ness." An effective way to counter this tendency is to generate alternative explanations. To generate alternative explanations, ask yourself these questions in response to your negative thoughts:

- *What's the worst-case scenario?*

- *What's the best-case scenario?*

- *What's the most likely scenario?*

- *What are at least three other possibilities?*

Anti-catastrophic thinking. When you feel anxious, your mind fills with catastrophic thoughts and images. *I'll be fired and jobless forever. I'll be mortified if I mess this up. No one will ever respect me.* One antidote is asking yourself a series of questions designed to "de-catastrophize" your thinking.

- *What is the worst that could happen?*

- *How likely is it that the worst would actually happen?*

- *What could I do to cope if that did occur?*

- *How often have I been right in the past when I predicted catastrophe?*

Image substitution. When you're feeling anxious, terrible images of the future flood your mind. For example, if you're worried about an upcoming presentation, you might picture yourself up at 4 am frantically trying to recover your slides from a crashed computer. You might see yourself sweaty and stuttering before the room.

When you look into the future, however, you are imagining something that hasn't happened yet. Things can—and often do—turn out very differently than we envision. When you're playing horror scenes in your mind, remember: you do have a choice. You don't have to choose to put energy into these thoughts. The only thing accomplished by imagining the worst in the future is making you miserable in the present. How about a more pleasant, enjoyable scene instead? Perhaps you could see yourself calmly answering a question from the crowd. Or maybe you could picture your coworkers clapping for you at the end of your talk. You could imagine your boss shaking your hand afterward and saying you did a great job. The next time you catch your mind flooded with negative images, try countering them with a more positive scene instead.

Let's take a look at how Maggie used these strategies to turn her thinking around, change how she felt, and take a step toward recovered productivity.

Maggie's Thought Sheet: Step Three

Situation	Feelings	Anxious Thoughts	Cognitive Distortions	Techniques	Rational Coping Responses
At our monthly meeting, my station manager reveals pending budget cuts and tells us that she'll be meeting with each of us individually to discuss our ideas for improving the station. She also scheduled weekly brainstorming meetings with the whole staff.	Anxious	I won't be able to think of anything useful.	Fortune telling, All-or-nothing thinking	Examine the evidence	I don't really know this for sure. Sometimes I do come up with useful suggestions.
		I should be coming up with better ideas.	Should statement, Discounting the positives	Examine the evidence	My ideas are sometimes well received, and, while I offer fewer opinions than some, I give more than others.
		If we all spend more time together, everyone will see that I'm not really competent.	Mind-reading, All-or-nothing thinking	Generate alternatives	While possible, a more likely scenario is that—good or bad—they'll think the same they always have of me.
		What if I'm fired? I'll be devastated.	"What-if?" thinking, Catastrophic thinking, Discounting coping skills	Anti-catastrophic thinking	This isn't likely, but if it did happen, my life wouldn't be over. I could look for another job.
		Maybe being fired would be better than having everyone at work thinking I'm a loser.	Mind-reading, discounting coping skills	Image substitution	I don't know that others think I'm a loser. I can picture myself coping with my anxiety rather than avoiding it.

As you can see from Maggie's thought sheet, she used a variety of different techniques to defeat her negative thoughts. You too may find that some strategies work better than others for certain types of thoughts or situations. Be sure to try them all to find out which ones work best for you.

Now it's your turn. Starting with your thought sheet, use the techniques listed to generate rational coping responses that dispute your negative thinking.

How did you do? Were you able to come up with more balanced ways to look at your fearful thoughts? Which techniques did you find most helpful? Continue to do this exercise whenever you find yourself procrastinating or when you feel anxious about something. Remember to try all the strategies at least once to find the ones that work best for you.

Step Four: Examine the Root of Your Fears

Now that you've learned to counter the anxious thoughts that arise and lead you to procrastinate, it's time to take a closer look at why succeeding matters so much to you. If you're like most people, you may not have taken the time to stop and think about why the idea of failing seems so scary to you. Failing is just bad, right? As much as this may feel like a universal truth, there are plenty of very successful people who disagree with you. Albert Einstein said, "Anyone who has never made a mistake has never tried anything new." Abraham Lincoln told us, "Success is going from failure to failure without losing your enthusiasm." And the list goes on and on. You need not look any farther than Google to find endless quotes on the importance of failure in life. If so many great minds believe that failing is an essential part of learning and success, then why does it feel so hard to accept it? The answer may be in your beliefs about what failure means to you or, perhaps more accurately, *about* you. Try the simple exercise below to get to the core of why failing (or succeeding) may be so terrifying to you.

EXERCISE: What Would It Mean?

Choose a thought from your sheets that you feel reflects your fear of failure (or fear of success) and write it in the space below.

Thought: _____

_____

Now ask yourself the following questions and write the answers in the space provided.

If this were true, why would it bother me? _____

_____

Okay, so what would that mean about me? _____

_____

If that were true, what would it mean? _____

_____

And why would that be so bad? _____

_____

Keep going as far as you can until you find the answer to why failing feels so catastrophic to you. You can use the questions that follow to help you. You've already learned to counter your fearful thoughts, but because they're a driving force behind your anxiety, figuring out what these thoughts actually *mean* to you will be critical in overcoming your fear and procrastination once and for all.

Getting to the Root of Your Fears

1. If this thought were true, why would it bother me?

2. What would this mean about me?

3. If that were true, what would it mean?

4. Why would that be so bad?

5. So, what would happen then?

6. Why would that matter?

7. What would that change?

_____

If you are having trouble with this investigation, take a look at Maggie's sheet below. Maggie chose the thought "I won't be able to think of anything useful."

Maggie's "What Would It Mean?" Exercise

Thought: _I won't be able to think of anything useful._ _____

If this were true, why would it bother me? _Everyone will think I'm not pulling my weight._

_____

Okay, so what would that mean about me? _I don't belong here._

_____

If that were true, what would it mean? _I'll never fit in anywhere._

_____

And why would that be so bad?   _No one will ever love me._

If you fear success, you might find Wayne's sheet more helpful. Wayne used this exercise to help him understand why getting a promotion felt so scary to him.

Wayne's "What Would It Mean?" Exercise

Thought: _I might get that promotion._

If this were true, why would it bother me? _I may not be able to handle the responsibility._

Okay, so what would that mean about me?   _I'm not as good as they think I am._

If that were true, what would it mean?   _I've gone as far as I can at work._

And why would that be so bad?   _It means I don't have the potential I hoped I had._

You can see from both Maggie and Wayne that our anxious thoughts often have a deeper significance. In this case, Maggie believes that failure at her job would reflect an underlying lack of worth and prevent her from ever being deserving of love. Wayne thinks that his success may eventually show that his full potential has been reached and is short of his expectations. The list that follows illustrates some common beliefs that anxious procrastinators hold about themselves and the world. Do any of these ring true for you? Did you come up with any of your own? If so, you can write them in the spaces provided.

Common Beliefs Behind Fear of Failure or Success

- I need approval from others to be worthwhile.

- How I do reflects how important I am.

- People will never accept me as I am.

- I need to do well to deserve love.

- Only successful people are worthy of respect.

- Love must be earned.

- I must succeed at everything to be a worthwhile person.

- I should always please others and live up to their expectations.

- _____

- _____

Once you pinpoint the beliefs behind your fears, you are ready to challenge them.

Use the strategies from Step Three to counter these beliefs and create healthier attitudes for yourself. In doing so, you will break free of the fears that hold you back and will propel yourself toward improved productivity.

Step Five: Practice Confronting Your Fear

Battling the fearful thoughts that lead to your anxiety and procrastination has put you on the right path, but in order to truly overcome your fear of failure and success you still need to put these changes into play in real life. One of the most effective ways for you to conquer your fear is simply to face it. Directly confronting your fears is called *exposure therapy* or *exposure and response prevention* (ERP). Of course, confronting the things you fear is a simple idea, but it's not easy. In fact, it can be terrifying. So, before you use exposure as a method to overcome your fears, it's important to understand how and why exposure works.

HABITUATION: WHY EXPOSURE WORKS

ERP has been studied extensively and has been found to be a highly effective treatment for anxiety. Research shows that if you engage in focused and repeated exposure to a thought or situation, your anxiety will decrease over time (Foa and Kozak 1986). This process is called *habituation*. It is our body's natural way of adjusting to repeated or prolonged contact with something.

For instance, think back to the first time you put on a watch. For a while, you were continually aware of the fact that you were wearing it. You may have even caught yourself adjusting the band or taking it off altogether. This constant readjustment and inconsistent contact prolonged your awareness of its presence. But once you left it alone for a time, your body began to habituate to this new object. Now you barely know it's there. Believe it or not, the same process of habituation occurs with anxiety.

For example, Maggie feared speaking up in meetings because she worried that her ideas would flop and she would be perceived as incompetent. With the new mandate put forth by her boss, however, Maggie now *had* to speak up to keep her job. She created the goal for herself that in each meeting she would offer at least one opinion or suggestion and then steeled herself to do it. She was sure that each meeting would be excruciating, but she was determined to stick with it. Then something unexpected happened...the more Maggie spoke, the more comfortable she became. She stuck faithfully to her goal and found that her anxiety decreased with each day. She began to fear less and less that she would be seen as a failure. Now that she was not avoiding her fears, her anxiety lessened (or habituated).

EXERCISE: Practice Confronting Your Fears

Each day choose one practice exposure to confront your fears. You can use the ideas in the lists that follow or come up with your own. Start by picking something small and work your way up to more anxiety-provoking situations. Whenever possible, try to perform the practice exposure repeatedly until it doesn't cause you much anxiety. Once you've mastered that, move on to something harder. Alternatively, pick a few exposures that cause you roughly the same amount of anxiety and rotate through them until you habituate. With practice on these small "failures" or "successes," you'll be facing down your bigger fears in no time!

Practice Failures

◆ Intentionally use an incorrect word in conversation.

◆ Drop something loudly at the cafeteria or a restaurant.

◆ Wish someone a good morning when it's afternoon.

◆ Give the wrong amount of money to a cashier or "forget" your wallet.

◆ Ask for directions to a street you are on.

◆ Allow your hand to tremble while holding a glass of water.

◆ Show up for an appointment on the wrong day.

◆ Enter a door incorrectly (push when it says "pull") in front of others.

◆ Ask an obvious customer for information in a store as if he or she works there.

◆ Mispronounce a word in conversation.

◆ _____

◆ _____

◆ _____

Practice Successes

◆ In a meeting, offer an answer you know is correct.

◆ Tell a random trivia fact to a friend or colleague.

◆ Volunteer to head up a project at work.

◆ Give a presentation in front of a group of coworkers.

◆ Share something you've succeeded on with a friend or family member.

◆   Simply say thank you to a compliment without qualifying it.

◆   _____

◆   _____

◆   _____

NEXT STEPS

After reading this chapter and completing the exercises, you should now recognize your fears of failure and success, be able to identify and counter the anxious thoughts that accompany them, and understand what those thoughts mean to you personally. If you haven't practiced countering your fearful thoughts and the beliefs you hold about them as well as confronting feared situations, take some time to go back and do that now. If you are feeling comfortable facing your fears of failure or success and challenging the anxious thoughts that accompany them, you are ready to move on. Use the strategies here along with those in the remainder of the book on your quest to overcome procrastination.

Key Points

◆   Fears of failure or success often underlie procrastination. Your beliefs about what succeeding or failing may mean about you can lead to worry, anxiety, and procrastination.

◆   Your thoughts play a key role in your mood. By changing your thinking, you can change how you feel.

◆   Finding the cognitive distortions in your thinking can help you come up with more rational coping responses to your fears.

◆   Confronting practice successes and failures can help you more comfortably face down your bigger fears.

5

Know That You Can Do It

It was Alisa's first day of college. She walked in and looked around at the noisy, crowded classroom. She noticed a few empty seats and chose one. She could feel butterflies in her stomach and sweat on her palms. She sat down and put her backpack next to her. She took out her notebook and a pen and smiled nervously at the student sitting next to her. He smiled back and said, "I hear this class is tough. The professor is really demanding." Alisa felt a lump build in her throat. She waited with anxious anticipation, eyeing the pile of syllabi on the professor's desk. As he started to hand them out, Alisa could feel her mind racing: "I hope there aren't any papers. I'm terrible at those. I can't write. I'm a horrible writer. I'll probably fail this class and flunk out my first semester." The person next to her passed Alisa a copy of the syllabus. She quickly thumbed through the pages, looking for the assignments. Her heart sank when she saw the final assignment: a twenty-page research paper. She felt filled with anxiety, dread, and fear.

When Alisa was confronted with a task—a term paper in this case—she experienced a flood of thoughts about her abilities to complete it. Alisa is not unique. When we're faced with a task or challenge, our beliefs about our ability to complete the task and achieve our desired results are activated. These thoughts reflect our self-efficacy. If you're struggling to overcome anxious procrastination, it's important to note that researchers have found a connection between our self-efficacy and our tendency to procrastinate (Tan et al. 2008; Steel 2007).

This chapter addresses doubts that you may have about your ability to effect change in a situation and your ability to function well regardless of external evaluation. We've included cognitive-therapy worksheets to track and challenge the negative beliefs that undermine your self-efficacy as well as CBT exercises to help you develop an accurate picture of your abilities.

MORE ABOUT SELF-EFFICACY

The term "self-efficacy" means your belief in your ability to complete a specific task or succeed in a particular situation (Bandura 1997). When we're confronted with a task, whether it's a presentation at work, a project for school, or a leaky faucet at home, we immediately assess our ability to accomplish the goal. Our minds scan the task, evaluate our skills, and match the two. The net result—our assessment of our skills as matched against a specific task—generates our sense of self-efficacy about that task. If we feel our skills are equal to or greater than the challenge, we have what's called *adequate* or *high self-efficacy*. If there's a discrepancy between our perceived abilities and the task—if we think our skills aren't adequate—then we have what's known as *low self-efficacy*.

Our beliefs about our abilities to complete a task play a key role in determining whether we take action and get it done or we procrastinate. If we have adequate or high self-efficacy about a specific task, then we often eagerly plunge forward. If we believe our abilities aren't up to snuff, we often shrink from the challenge. For example, imagine that through hard work and practice, you developed great skill at cooking. At the same time, you never developed your singing voice. Now picture yourself at a party. In the kitchen, the host is whipping up some last-minute snacks and would like some help. In the living room, there's karaoke. Where do you think you'll go? If you're like most, since your self-efficacy in the kitchen is much higher, you'll wander in there.

You might have noticed that we're talking about your *beliefs* about your abilities to complete a task. It's really these beliefs—not our abilities themselves—that play a role in procrastination. What we believe often becomes a self-fulfilling prophecy. It's as Henry Ford said, "If you think you can or you think you can't, either way you are right." As you'll learn in the upcoming section, our beliefs about our abilities are often distorted. Many people who procrastinate *believe* they are incapable when in fact their performance is more than adequate. These negative beliefs destroy your self-efficacy and lead to procrastination.

Procrastination, in turn, further tears down your self-efficacy. If you avoid tasks or put them off until the last minute, you'll convince yourself that you lack the needed skills. Procrastination can also negatively affect your self-confidence or your general sense of your overall capabilities. People who have a healthy self-efficacy have come by it honestly. By completing tasks over and over, they have a strong foundational sense of "Yes, I can do it." They have high self-efficacy and good self-confidence. If we have low self-efficacy and we procrastinate, the result is a vicious cycle—we believe we're no good at something, so we avoid it, which prevents us from disproving this belief and building our skills. In the process, our self-confidence is destroyed as well. You'll find as you work through the steps in this next section that your self-efficacy grows and, as a bonus, you'll find your overall sense of self-confidence blossoms as well.

HOW TO IMPROVE YOUR SELF-EFFICACY

Now that you understand self-efficacy and the key role it plays in procrastination, let's talk about some ways you can enhance your own efficacy. In this section, you'll find a five-step plan to help you increase your ability to get things done.

Our five-step plan consists of:

1. Identifying your negative thoughts

2. Identifying any distortions in your thinking

3. Replacing negative thoughts with rational responses

4. Conducting an experiment

5. Improving your skills

Step One: Identify Your Negative Thoughts

The first step in increasing your sense of being able to accomplish tasks and decreasing procrastination is to identify the thoughts that are eroding your confidence. Why are these thoughts so important? They're crucial for two reasons. The first is that they profoundly influence how you feel. Remember Alisa, the college student at the beginning of this chapter? When she was faced with a challenging paper for school, she was flooded with negative thoughts about her ability to complete the task. Her mind filled with thoughts such as "I'm a horrible writer" and "I'm terrible at papers." These thoughts caused Alisa to feel anxious and depressed.

The second reason these thoughts are so important is that they also have a huge influence on what you will do. Let's think of Alisa again. With thoughts such as hers, how do you think she's likely to act in that situation? In all likelihood, she'll procrastinate on her paper or avoid it all together. She might even drop the class and try to fill all her classes with those that don't require papers. However, since papers are common, she may have difficulty finding classes without them and end up dropping out completely, never fulfilling her dream of earning a college degree.

In any given situation, people tend to *think, feel,* and *do*. Considering these three factors—what you think, how you feel, and what you do—is a good way to understand your behavior. This relationship between your thoughts, your emotions, and your behaviors is central to understanding self-efficacy and understanding yourself in any situation. Remember, the key to enhancing your self-efficacy is to change the way you think. As a result, you'll feel more motivated and will behave in a more productive way. Later on in this section you'll learn methods for dealing with these thoughts. For now, let's focus on identifying your negative thoughts.

For the worksheet that follows, think of a time recently that you were faced with a task and felt defeated before you started. What was the situation, the task you faced? What were you feeling? What was going through your mind? List on the worksheet the trigger (the task that seemed daunting), the thoughts you had, and your feelings. For now ignore the other three columns. If you'd like to see an example, check out Alisa's worksheet that follows.

Thought Sheet

Situation	Feelings	Anxious Thoughts	Cognitive Distortions	Techniques	Rational Coping Responses

Alisa's Thought Sheet: Step One

Situation	Feelings	Anxious Thoughts
A twenty-page paper due for class	*Anxious* *Depressed*	*I'm a terrible at papers.* *I can't write.* *I'm a horrible writer.* *I'll probably flunk out of college my first semester.*

Step Two: Identify Distortions

In chapter 4, you learned about cognitive distortions. You'll recall that a thought is considered distorted if it's erroneous, faulty, or illogical in some way. Often our thoughts about our ability to complete a task are distorted, leading to unnecessarily harsh self-evaluation and anxious procrastination. The most common cognitive distortions associated with low self-efficacy include:

◆ **All-or-Nothing Thinking:** You view things in extreme categories. You see tasks as either something you can or can't do. Any shades of gray are filtered out.

◆ **Overgeneralization:** Here, you make broad, global inferences based on few events. For example, if you're late for one meeting, you might think, "I can't ever be on time."

◆ **Fortune Telling:** Fortune telling means making predictions about the future, usually negative ones. Thinking you'll certainly fail at a task, that you can't do it, that others will be disappointed are all examples of fortune telling.

◆ **Discounting the Positives:** When you discount the positives, you insist that the good parts don't count. For example, when Jesse received positive feedback from a supervisor on a project, he thought, *Anyone could've done that.*

◆ **Mental Filtering:** This means picking a negative part of a situation and dwelling on it. For instance, if you have difficulty with an aspect of your job, you might focus on that "failure" and feel it represents your overall performance.

Even though these cognitive distortions are the most common, you might find any one of the ten cognitive distortions from chapter 4 in your negative thoughts.

Next take a look at your list of negative thoughts on your thought sheet. Now look at the checklist of cognitive distortions. On your thought sheet, list any distortions you see in your thoughts.

Alisa's Thought Sheet: Step Two

Situation	Feelings	Anxious Thoughts	Cognitive Distortions
A twenty-page paper due for class	*Anxious* *Depressed*	*I'm terrible at papers.*	*All-or-nothing thinking, Discounting the positives, Mental Filtering*
		I can't write.	*All-or-nothing thinking;*
		I'm a horrible writer.	*All-or-nothing thinking, Discounting the positives, Mental filtering*
		I'll probably flunk out of college my first semester.	*Fortune telling*

Step Three: Replace Negative Thoughts with Rational Responses

Now that you've identified the negative thoughts that lead you to avoidance and procrastination, you're ready for the key next step. Remember, there's a direct connection among your thoughts, feelings, and behaviors. By changing the way you view yourself and modifying your perspective on challenging situations, you'll feel more confident and you'll be more likely to complete the task at hand.

In chapter 4, you learned several ways to challenge your negative thoughts. These techniques include:

◆ Examining the evidence

◆ Generating alternatives

◆ Anti-catastrophic thinking

◆ Image substitution

You can use one or more of these techniques to challenge your negative thoughts and turn your thinking around.

Returning to your thought sheet, select one of your negative thoughts from step one. Since you've already identified distortions in this thought, you're ready to replace it with a more realistic, rational response. Use one or more of the techniques listed above and described in chapter 4 to generate new ways of looking at your skills and the challenge you face. Write these down in the Rational Coping Responses column.

Alisa's Thought Sheet: Step Three

Situation	Feelings	Anxious Thoughts	Cognitive Distortions	Techniques	Rational Coping Responses
A twenty-page paper due for class	Anxious Depressed	I'm terrible at papers.	All or nothing, discounting positives, mental filter	Examine the evidence	I find papers a challenge, but when I complete them, they usually turn out fine.
		I can't write.	All or nothing	Generate alternatives	I'm capable of writing.
		I'm a horrible writer.	All or nothing, discounting the positives	Examine the evidence	I've earned good grades on papers.
		I'll probably flunk out of college my first semester.	Fortune telling	Anti-catastrophic thinking	I'll only flunk out if I don't turn in assignments.

Step Four: Conduct an Experiment

When we have a thought—positive or negative—about our abilities to complete a task, we often accept it as truth without questioning it. Alisa really believed her thoughts were true, that she was in fact a horrible writer. And the rub is that our thoughts often become a self-fulfilling prophecy. By telling ourselves we can't—without questioning it—we usually resort to avoidance. This avoidance confirms and strengthens our belief that we really are inept. One way to deal with self-defeating negative thoughts about your self-efficacy is to put them to the test by conducting an experiment. In this way, you can check the validity of your negative belief.

Lars was a twenty-five-year-old graduate student who had put off studying for an exam. He called our office the afternoon of the exam in a panic. It was three o'clock, the test was at six. "I'm going to skip the midterm and drop the course. If I take it, I'll fail for sure. I haven't studied nearly enough." Lars took his thought "I'll fail for sure" as fact, and his immediate reaction was a surge of panic and plans to skip the exam. However, after some urging, he decided to view his thought as a hypothesis and conduct an experiment instead. Lars agreed to take the exam, despite his fears. When he got back the results, he was stunned to see his grade: B+. By following through, he was able to test and challenge his negative thought rather than assume it was a fact. He earned a good grade and averted dropping out of the class. As a bonus, his self-efficacy improved as well.

EXERCISE: Conduct Your Own Experiment

The next time you're faced with a task and you feel a flood of negative thoughts pulling you to avoid or procrastinate, try giving the task a shot instead. Put your negative thoughts to the test to see if they're really true or if they represent distorted negative thinking. Like Lars, you might surprise yourself and do better than you think.

Step Five: Improve Your Skills

If you use step four frequently, you'll develop a more accurate picture of your abilities. Your self-efficacy will climb, and your tendency to resort to procrastination will decline. As you review the results of your experiments, you'll find that you were accurate in some things you weren't good at and inaccurate in others. The result is that you'll achieve a more balanced and clearer view of yourself.

Most of the time, our thoughts about our ability to complete a task are distorted and inaccurate. We judge ourselves too harshly and negatively. We convince ourselves we're just not good enough, so we worry, avoid, and procrastinate, thinking our skills just aren't up to snuff. Sometimes, though, our skills do fall short of what's required, and we put things off as a result. In those instances, it can be a tremendous help to focus on building the skills you need to succeed. Armed with your new abilities, you'll feel calmer and more confident, eager to plunge forward and get things done.

First, let's take a moment and pinpoint your areas of strength. Below, list five areas in which you are strong.

Things I'm Good At

- _____
- _____
- _____
- _____
- _____

As you do so, you might ask yourself how often you procrastinate on these tasks. Chances are, you're eager to do them.

Next, go ahead and list areas you *think* you're not so good in but in which you really do just fine. These areas will be places where you commonly procrastinate, though your skills are more than adequate to get the job done. These areas can be a bit challenging to identify. To tease them out, think of times when you completed tasks from this category and did a good job, despite your beliefs. Or consider the views of other people. Are there tasks you aren't so confident about but for which you've received positive feedback from others?

Things I Mistakenly Believe I Don't Do Well

◆ _____

◆ _____

◆ _____

◆ _____

◆ _____

Take a look at the list above. What are your thoughts about those areas? It might be helpful for you to identify and challenge your negative thoughts about your skills in those areas to see if you are thinking of them in a distorted light. Use the strategies you've learned to identify any cognitive distortions and replace negative interpretations with a more realistic view.

Like everyone, you may also have areas where your skills really could use some work. Now let's take a look at tasks in which you could use improvement. These may be things that you haven't had much exposure to, haven't had the chance to practice, or just don't understand well.

Things I'm Not So Good At

◆ _____

◆ _____

◆ _____

◆ _____

◆ _____

Take a look at these items. As an exercise, choose one and circle it. Rate your competency in this area on a 1-to-10 scale, where 1 is the worst and 10 is expert. How good do you think you are at this thing right now? Since these are things you're not so good at, the number may be pretty low. Now brainstorm for a few minutes on how you could improve. You might list ways such as taking a class, getting a tutor, or reading a how-to book. List your ideas below.

What I Can Do to Improve

◆ _____

◆ _____

◆ _____

◆ _____

◆ _____

Once you've identified ways to improve your skills in the area you selected, it's time to get to work. Take the steps necessary to get better. To assess your progress, you can rate your skill regularly on the 1-to-10 scale. Keep working at it until your abilities reach at least 7 or 8. Make your weakness into a strength. You'll find you engage in anxious procrastination in that area much less as a result.

Jim, a client of ours, used this step to great benefit. Jim came to therapy at our practice to overcome his fear of public speaking. Jim had suffered from this fear almost his whole life. He sought treatment at 47, and the last time he could remember speaking in public was at a presentation in the eighth grade. In every situation since then, Jim had found an excuse to decline speaking invitations or had gotten so anxious and put off preparation so long that he ended up calling in sick on the day of the talk. All in all, Jim had over thirty years of fearing and avoiding public speaking. As you can imagine, in addition to Jim's fear, he just wasn't very good at giving a presentation because he hadn't had any practice with it. In therapy, Jim brainstormed ways he could improve his skills. He found ways to get practice speaking in public on a regular basis, like introducing himself to others, volunteering to head a committee at his daughter's school, and joining his local Toastmaster's International group. As his skills grew and his anxiety diminished, Jim felt more and more confident talking in front of a group. His self-efficacy soared and his avoidance of public speaking declined. His boss noticed his new confidence and skills as well, and Jim earned a long-coveted promotion as a result.

Like Jim, one of the best ways to improve your skills is to practice what you *aren't* good at. Remember, our self-efficacy often puts us on autopilot—sending us off to the tasks we're skilled at and encouraging avoidance of tasks we find difficult. By making a conscious effort to improve skills that need work, you'll further bolster your self-efficacy and lessen anxious procrastination.

NEXT STEPS

Now you understand the concept of self-efficacy and the role it plays in procrastination. You've also learned and practiced a five-step plan for boosting your self-efficacy. You've identified negative thoughts that sap your self-efficacy and you've learned specific ways to challenge them. You've also practiced testing your negative thoughts and considered ways to enhance your skills. Armed with this new confidence, you're ready to proceed on to the next steps in defeating your anxious procrastination, like addressing perfectionism, setting achievable goals, and developing better time-management skills.

Key Points

◆ Self-efficacy means your perception of your ability to achieve a goal or accomplish a task. If you believe your skills are equal to the task, you have what's known as adequate or high self-efficacy. If you think you aren't up to snuff on a particular challenge, you have what's known as low self-efficacy.

◆ Research has shown a connection between low self-efficacy and procrastination. As a general rule, if we don't believe we can do something, we will put it off or avoid it altogether.

◆ By following our five-step plan (identifying your thoughts, identifying distortions, developing rational responses, conducting experiments, and getting better), you can enhance your self-efficacy and decrease your tendency to rely on procrastination.

6

Accept Imperfection and Uncertainty

Perfectionism is the culprit behind avoidance and delay for many procrastinators, although they rarely recognize it right off the bat. Many of our clients come to therapy feeling disorganized, discouraged, and as though they never do anything right. These folks would never independently identify themselves as perfectionists, but ironically, it is often their high standards and impossible goals that keep them stuck. You may be thinking, *Why do I need to read this chapter? I'm not a perfectionist. I never do anything perfectly!* Read on, though, and you may be surprised to find out how much perfectionism influences procrastination—even your own.

John ran his own small business. He was bright, affable, and initially well liked by his clients. He landed lucrative accounts with ease and had the skill and talent to manage them well. From the outside things seemed under control, but one look at John's office told the real story: half-written proposals, piles of unpaid bills, stacks of motivational books, and countless messages from clients wondering when their projects would be completed. John blamed these "failures" on his motivation, his work ethic, and his ability, and he vowed to set a higher standard for himself, work harder, and overcome his procrastination. But, in truth, it was his high standards that led him to procrastinate in the first place. John was a perfectionist. He spent hours writing and rewriting already-acceptable proposals in attempts to make them perfect and then never finished them. He read book after book on the right way to run a successful business. But because he could never find the perfect set of suggestions, he never implemented any of them.

If you asked John, he would say he needed to be *more* perfect, not less. But the futility of trying to live up to impossible standards actually led him to be less productive, more stressed, and, ultimately, less successful. In this chapter, you'll learn more about perfectionism, how it may contribute to your procrastination, and how being more "average" may actually improve your performance.

WHAT IS A PERFECTIONIST?

When most people think of perfectionists, they imagine people like Felix Unger or Martha Stewart, with their neatly pressed trousers, gourmet meals, and dislike of dust. But, really, to be a perfectionist you need only to view perfection as the goal—not necessarily achieve it. Your house may be a mess because you won't implement an organizational system until you can find the "right" one, or you may fail to file your taxes until you can find every receipt you may need. Perfectionists strive for perfection and view anything less as unacceptable; however, they often fall short. In fact, the quest for perfection rarely results in success. It does result in more stress, higher anxiety (Stoeber, Feast, and Hayward 2009), and decreased performance (Sub and Prabha 2003). Things get put off. Piles build up. Decisions don't get made. The pressure of trying to achieve unachievable goals and answering unanswerable questions is overwhelming; the pursuit of perfection inevitably ends up sapping motivation and leading to nothing being done at all.

In the next sections, you'll learn how to identify your own perfectionism and begin accepting the imperfection and uncertainty inherent in life. As a result, you'll be more relaxed, realistic, and productive while your urge to procrastinate fades.

OVERCOMING THE NEED TO BE PERFECT

Still not convinced that you're a perfectionist? Answer the following questions as truthfully as you can:

Y N   Do your standards overwhelm you more often than motivate you?

Y N   Do you expect more from yourself than you do from others?

Y N   Do you find that it takes you much longer than others to complete tasks?

Y N   Do you put things off until the time is "right"?

Y N   Do mistakes bother you excessively, or do you view them as failures?

Y N   Do you spend more time planning for projects than actively working on them?

Y N   Do you feel that whatever you do is not quite good enough?

Y N   Do you have trouble adjusting your standards to fit time or resource constraints?

Y N   Do you do things out of a sense of duty rather than enjoyment or satisfaction?

Y N   Do you tend to do busywork when faced with a difficult task?

Y N   Do questions without "right" answers or uncertain outcomes make you anxious?

Y N   When faced with a decision, do you find yourself paralyzed by the options?

If you answered yes to any of these questions, you may be a closet perfectionist. If you answered yes to many of them, you probably already know that your perfectionism interferes with your productivity. In either case, you may find the steps in this chapter useful. They are:

1. Challenging perfectionistic beliefs

2. Banishing the shoulds

3. Being average

4. Tolerating uncertainty

Step One: Challenge Perfectionistic Beliefs

As you've learned from the previous two chapters, what you tell yourself has a profound impact on how you feel. Perfectionists often learn at a young age that being "the best" is crucial and that every problem has a "right" answer. They think that in order to be loved or accepted, one must be special or perfect. For them, failing at a specific task means failing as a person. To a perfectionist, coming in second is the same as finishing last. If you identify with these beliefs, it may be time to honestly ask yourself if thinking this way really does motivate you to be better or whether it just adds worry, stress, and anxiety that lead to the opposite outcome—procrastination.

Phil grew up in a family that stressed the importance of academic excellence and required his participation in sports. Despite being a strong student, he was often "grounded" to do homework while his friends were out socializing. And though he was the star player on his basketball team, his father could often be heard bellowing criticism from the stands. As an adult, Phil carried those experiences with him. He felt that nothing he did was ever good enough and that nothing short of the best was acceptable. Though he graduated from law school and worked for a mid-level firm, he felt like a failure because he wasn't a star lawyer. If questioned, he would insist that unless he could achieve greatness, none of his hard work mattered. Phil expected his briefs to be perfect, his arguments airtight. He spent hours trying to find research to back up a single case point and, as a result, he perpetually lagged behind in his work, rarely finishing projects. Because he often couldn't decide the right direction to take his argument, he ended up going nowhere.

Look back to the list of cognitive distortions in chapter 4 and see if you can identify any in Phil's thinking.

Thought	Distortion(s)
Anything short of greatness is failure.	_____
It would be awful to be just average.	_____
A mistake in my work invalidates the whole brief.	_____

If you think that Phil engages in all-or-nothing and catastrophic thinking as well as mental filtering, you're correct. These are common cognitive distortions for perfectionists. As you learned in chapter 4, Phil could use such strategies as examining the evidence, generating alternatives, applying anti-catastrophic thinking, or image substitution to challenge his distorted thinking. Let's take a look.

Phil's Thought Sheet

Situation	Feelings	Anxious Thoughts	Cognitive Distortions	Techniques	Rational Coping Responses
Preparing a brief for a big case.	*Anxious*	*Anything short of greatness is failure.*	*All-or-nothing thinking*	*Examine the evidence*	*While plenty of people may not reach what I might call greatness, they still could be important and contribute a lot.*
		It would be awful to be just average.	*Catastrophic thinking*	*Anti-catastrophic thinking*	*Maybe I could cope with it. Plenty of my average friends and colleagues seem pretty happy.*
		A mistake in my work would invalidate the whole thing.	*Mental filtering*	*Generate alternatives*	*There are often errors in projects this large, but the overall product is still worthwhile.*

PRACTICE CHALLENGING PERFECTIONISTIC THOUGHTS

Now that you've seen how Phil was able to identify the cognitive distortions in his thinking, challenge them, and generate more helpful coping responses, use the thought record below to challenge any perfectionistic thinking of your own.

Thought Sheet

Situation	Feelings	Anxious Thoughts	Cognitive Distortions	Techniques	Rational Coping Responses

Were you able to find examples of perfectionistic distortions in your thinking? Did you come up with more balanced ways to look at these unrealistic standards? Which techniques did you find most helpful? Continue to use those techniques whenever you find yourself anxious or procrastinating.

Step Two: Banish the Shoulds

You may remember "should statements" from the list of cognitive distortions in chapter 4. Recall that should statements are rigid rules about how things "should" be. Directing a should toward yourself leads you to feel guilty, regretful, or inadequate. Shoulds aimed at others generally lead to anger or disappointment. Shoulds are very difficult, often impossible, to live up to, so peppering yourself with these kinds of expectations makes you feel like a failure.

You might be wondering why shoulds were not just included in step one—they *are* cognitive distortions, after all. The reason is this: shoulds are so prominent for perfectionists that we simply felt that they deserved their own step. They probably deserve their own book! Listen to any perfectionist and you'll hear a litany of shoulds:

- I should never make mistakes.

- I should be the best at whatever I do.

- I should know the answer.

- I should be able to do things easily.

- I should be the perfect friend/spouse/worker.

- I should always be charming and funny.

- I should always get things done on time.

- I should never need help.

- I should not reveal weaknesses to others.

Are any of these beliefs in your repertoire? How do you think they affect your performance and productivity? If you answered that they motivate you to excel and be better, stop and really think about it—then ask yourself again. Shoulds almost always lead to frustration, disappointment, and guilt simply because they are so difficult to live up to. Who can possibly do all the things they "should" do? And who gets to decide what things qualify as musts anyway? I guess most of us could agree that we should breathe, should feed and clothe our children, and should not intentionally harm others. Beyond that, however, it's pretty subjective. Making most tasks into shoulds is really not appropriate; yet when we tell ourselves we should do something, we act as though it's the literal truth.

EXERCISE: Get Rid of Your Shoulds

The goal in this step is to minimize your list of shoulds to only the most fundamental of tasks and behaviors. Going forward, try to eradicate the word "should" from your vocabulary. If you catch yourself using it, try to substitute one of the following instead:

- I may benefit from…

- I'd prefer…

- It may be to my advantage to…

- I want to…

- I may feel better if…

- I wish…

- It would be nice if…

To do this may take a lot of practice—shoulds can be pretty ingrained—so keep at it. If you are afraid to try, worried that your performance may further falter if you no longer use shoulds to whip yourself into shape, then just give it a shot for one week. Our prediction is that without the guilt, frustration, and resentment that shoulds evoke, you'll be free to accomplish things because you *want* to, not because you should. We expect your productivity will soar, not suffer. You "should" give it a try!

Step Three: Be Average

As a perfectionist, you may have grown up thinking that being "just average" is terrible and something to be actively avoided. You might have learned from your parents or teachers, from television, or maybe from your own experience that mistakes are shameful and embarrassing, that being the best is the only acceptable outcome. However your perfectionistic beliefs developed, if you look at them closely it is easy to find the flaws in that line of thinking. To begin, there can only be one best anything, by definition. So anyone else, no matter how worthy or bright, becomes the loser. If you don't see a problem with that, ask the Vice President or any Olympic silver medalist—they may have something to say about it! Much is accomplished in our world by the second-, fifth-, and two-hundredth-place finishers.

More importantly, though, this view is not useful. It generates an awful lot of pressure on you and can lead to such intense focus on not failing that you avoid taking risks and therefore make no gains—quite the opposite of the intended outcome. You can accomplish the façade of a perfect record by procrastinating; delay can protect you by keeping you from making mistakes that would expose you as average, but it also ties you up in knots, never letting you learn, grow, or succeed.

So what's the answer? Shine by embracing the average that most of us are. Enjoy the freedom that lowering your standards can bring. Allow yourself to take risks and possibly make mistakes. The next time you find yourself procrastinating because you're looking for the right answer or perfect strategy, shoot for average instead.

EXERCISE: Practice Being Average

Pick a task or a decision that's been looming, one that you've been avoiding. Instead of trying to put together something amazing or considering every possible angle, try to make it just "okay." If it's cleaning out your closet, don't worry about purging every pair of pants that no longer fits—just get most of them. If it's making a presentation at work, don't stress over hitting every possible point. Just hit most of them. If it's deciding which microwave to buy, pick one based on just what you know now. Aim for better than worst but less than first and see what happens!

How'd you do? Were you able to resist the urge to fix things until they met your standards? Did it feel uncomfortable to do things imperfectly or make a decision quickly? If so, don't worry—it will get easier with practice. You may be thinking, *But I don't want average to get comfortable! I don't want to make uninformed decisions.* If so, ask yourself how long you'd been putting off that task or decision before this exercise. And is it finished now? Only you can decide for yourself whether pretty good and finished is better than perfect but never done. If you decide the former, continue to use this strategy with any tasks or decisions you notice your perfectionism stalling or any time you find yourself procrastinating.

Step Four: Tolerate Uncertainty

What is uncertainty? *Uncertainty* is the state that exists when the outcome of something is unclear. If you think about it, this means anything in life. In fact, everything you face on a daily basis is uncertain. From the alarm clock ringing on time to having a rare but fatal allergic reaction when our head hits the goose-down pillow at night, we can never really be sure what will—or will not—happen each day. Uncertainty is just part of life.

As a perfectionist, however, you may try desperately to assert control over life or at least to continue the illusion that things are really within your control. Many of us don't relish uncertainty, but it seems that perfectionists have more trouble than others with accepting its inevitability. You feel you must know how things will turn out. The trouble is, you can't. No one has a crystal ball. Could your idea flop? Sure. Could you disappoint someone? It happens. Will you regret painting your living room that color? Maybe. Up until now, you may have used procrastination as a way to avoid facing the reality that we just don't know. You'll never know if your idea would flop, because you didn't offer it. Avoiding risks provides you with certainty. You don't need to worry as much about how things will turn out because, if you procrastinate, you already know—not well.

And, amazingly, some perfectionists would actually prefer a known negative outcome to uncertainty. That's where procrastination comes in handy. When you don't leave yourself enough time to do a good job, the result will almost certainly be a disappointment—but it will be an *expected* disappointment. Somehow, an expected failure is easier to cope with than a valiant effort with uncertain results. That way, you can take solace in the failed result not being a *true* reflection of your ability. You can tell yourself that you could have done much better if you'd only given yourself enough time. As comfortable as these old strategies may be, it's time to stop hiding behind them. Start developing a comfort level with the uncertain possibilities we face every day and, as a result, diminish your need to procrastinate.

EXERCISE: Practice Tolerating Uncertainty

The next time you find yourself procrastinating or worrying about the uncertain outcome of a task, decision, or event, stifle your urge to procrastinate and instead accept what is real—that you truly don't know for sure what the outcome will be. By accepting the doubt that is inherent in life, you will eliminate your need to procrastinate and allow yourself to excel. Practice the statements below and learn to become more comfortable with the surprises life brings:

- ◆ I'll never know for sure.

- ◆ Maybe it will, maybe it won't.

- ◆ I can't predict the future.

- ◆ I'll cope with things as they happen.

- ◆ Risk is a part of life—nothing ventured, nothing gained.

- ◆ I can't be absolutely certain either way.

- ◆ Anything is possible.

NEXT STEPS

After reading this chapter and completing the exercises, you should now know whether or not you suffer from perfectionism, be able to challenge any perfectionistic beliefs, and be on your way to achieving comfort with imperfection and uncertainty. If you haven't rid yourself of shoulds or still need to practice being average, take the next week or two to do that. Then use these abilities along with the upcoming strategies to continue becoming more comfortable with the imperfection and uncertainty inherent in life, and continue overcoming your procrastination.

Key Points

◆ Procrastinators rarely recognize themselves as perfectionists, but unrealistically high goals and standards are often behind procrastination.

◆ Challenging perfectionistic beliefs and ridding yourself of shoulds can pave the way to decreased stress and improved productivity.

◆ While perfectionists have difficulty with the idea of being average, trying *less* can actually lead you to achieve more.

◆ Uncertainty is a part of life and tolerating it is a skill that, when developed, allows you to take risks and put fewer things off.

Focus on the Now

Millie stared blankly at her desk, her eyes seemingly focused on the project before her but her thoughts far away. Images flooded her mind—the conference room filled with clients, her boss shaking his head disapprovingly, her colleagues looking away, embarrassed. Millie's palms were sweaty and her heart raced as this scene flashed through her mind. She looked at the stack of papers on her desk and couldn't even imagine how to begin. Her mind was too occupied with thoughts of failure, disappointment, and humiliation. The longer she sat there, the more anxious she became; and the more her anxiety escalated, the more vivid these images and thoughts became. Finally, she couldn't stand it anymore. Despite her looming deadline, she pushed her chair back from her desk, grabbed her coat, and left the office.

As you are well aware by now, anxiety is a vicious cycle and our thoughts play a critical role in whether that anxiety spirals out of control or simply passes through. For anxious procrastinators, the focus on embarrassing past failures or feared future screw-ups feeds anxiety, allowing it to escalate and, ultimately, paralyze productivity. In this chapter, you'll learn how to practice an approach called "mindfulness," which can help you remove yourself from this anxiety spiral and break the cycle of fear that leads you to avoid and procrastinate.

WHAT IS MINDFULNESS?

Being *mindful* means staying in the present—paying attention, on purpose, to the moment you are in without judging it (Kabat-Zinn 1990). The first goal of mindfulness is to learn how to focus on the present moment rather than letting thoughts stray to the past or the future. When you notice your mind wandering off, you bring your attention back to the present moment—the only one that truly matters. With some practice, mindfulness can help you to be more aware of your thoughts, emotions, and bodily sensations in the present. The second goal of mindfulness is then to allow these experiences to happen without judging them, pushing them away, or getting trapped in anxiety, guilt, worry, or remorse.

Mindfulness and Anxiety

Recent studies have found mindfulness-based therapies to be very effective in decreasing anxiety (Kim et al. 2009; Evans et al. 2008), worry, and stress (Craigie et al. 2008). It's harder to feel anxious about the past or worry about the future if you are rooted in the present. As you know, procrastination is often linked to worry about the future and fear of not living up to expectations. Anxious procrastinators beat themselves up about past imperfections and worry about future performance and potential failures. The moment-to-moment, nonjudgmental awareness of mindfulness encourages compassion and self-acceptance—it runs entirely counter to the usual attitudes of the anxious procrastinator. Mindfulness decreases anxiety, and when anxiety is lowered, avoidance diminishes and tasks get completed.

We've talked a lot in earlier chapters about thoughts and their capacity to lead to anxiety. Anxious thoughts result in anxiety, which leads to more anxious thoughts and more anxiety. And the more you try to avoid those thoughts, the more they get stuck. It's a paralyzing cycle, and avoidance is a natural though ultimately unhelpful response, stymieing creativity and productivity. Being mindful does not mean getting rid of anxious thoughts and feelings but instead recognizing them as temporary and fleeting. You can use mindfulness to change the way you experience these thoughts and emotions, understanding that they are momentary, will pass, and do not require a response. In this way, you can stop the cycle of anxiety and your reaction of avoidance and procrastination. Learning to allow your thoughts to happen without judging or reacting to them takes away their power and leaves you free to be present in the moment and to act in the now.

LEARNING TO BE MINDFUL

The beauty of being mindful is that you can do it anywhere. To begin, however, you may find that designating a specific time and place to practice may benefit you. A quiet, comfortable place that you've designated for practice will help you to stay focused on your task. Similarly, making a regular time in your schedule to practice will increase your odds of success. Try to pick a time when you won't be interrupted, and try to keep it generally around the same time each day. You may need to experiment to find the place and time that work best for you, so don't worry if it doesn't feel right at first.

For example, Millie decided that her favorite chair in the living room would be her best spot to practice in. The room was pleasant and sunny and, because she lived alone, quiet. A morning person, Millie decided to choose early morning as her practice time. She felt that using mindfulness first thing in the morning would also help to put her in a less anxious frame of mind and start her day off right. She set a goal of practicing every morning (but realized that the goal may not turn out to be realistic) and decided to give herself two "free passes" each week to use when needed. Think about what may work best for you, and use the spaces below to record where and when you will begin your practice.

Where I will practice mindfulness: _____

When I will practice mindfulness: _____

Now that you have chosen your place and time, use the steps that follow to get you started on the path. The steps are:

1. Breathe mindfully.

2. Eat mindfully.

3. Make everyday tasks mindful.

4. Watch your thoughts pass through.

5. Center yourself throughout the day.

As you practice the mindfulness exercises in this chapter, you may find that you'll enjoy it so much that you'll want to do it more. You can find more resources at the end of the chapter to help you find more information and additional ways to practice.

Step One: Breathe Mindfully

Awareness of breathing is a common and simple mindfulness exercise. Breathing is fundamental to life, but we are rarely aware of it. Practicing mindful breathing engages you in the present moment and enables you to refocus when you notice you are distracted. Breathing mindfully allows you to let thoughts and emotions come and go without judging or getting caught up in them. With practice, eventually you can breathe mindfully anywhere, but in the beginning you may find it easier to do in the place and at the time you have chosen.

EXERCISE: Mindful Breathing

1. Minimize distractions by turning off the television and phone. Let others know not to interrupt you for at least twenty minutes. Then sit in a comfortable position in your chosen spot. Put both feet on the floor and be aware of your posture, aligning your back, neck, and head.

2. Close your eyes and focus your attention on breathing. Feel the sensations of air entering and leaving your body. Feel your stomach expanding as you breathe in and falling as you exhale. If you want, you may say or think *in* as you inhale and *out* as you exhale to stay focused.

3. Allow each breath to come and go—do not try to control it. If your mind begins to wander, gently bring your attention back to breathing. Forget the next breath or your last one; focus on only the current breath.

4. Don't worry if you are doing it "right." It is human nature to evaluate but, no matter where or how often your mind wanders, simply refocus on your breaths without judgment.

5. Keep practicing until the end of your chosen time, whether it's five minutes or twenty. Gently open your eyes, notice how you feel, and then move on. As you begin to feel comfortable with the exercise, you can use it anytime throughout the day to refocus yourself.

If you choose, you can record your breathing practices on the sheet below. Remember, however, that each practice is its own. Do not compare or judge but instead focus on the present and let go of evaluation.

Mindful-Breathing Practice Sheet

Date/Time	Length of Practice	Notes/Thoughts

Step Two: Eat Mindfully

Most people eat automatically—in the car, in front of the television, at their desk. Like breathing, eating is central to our survival, but we rarely notice the experience. Think back to your last meal and answer the following questions:

What did you eat? _____

Where did you eat? _____

What else were you doing? _____

Who else was there? _____

What were you thinking about? _____

How did the food look? _____

How did it smell? _____

How did it taste? _____

Many people have little troubling answering the first four questions but have great difficulty with the rest. They may remember what they ate and the details of their eating environment but very little about the eating experience itself. Paying attention to the activity of eating is an opportunity to connect to the present moment and to slow down and notice a habit that has become automatic. Learning to really notice automatic actions like eating will make it easier for you to become more aware of habits you've developed that contribute to your procrastination.

EXERCISE: Mindful Eating

1. Choose a mealtime or use the time you've chosen to practice mindfulness to have a meal or snack. As with breathing practice, sit comfortably, with good posture, in a place where you won't be distracted by others or the television, phone, or radio.

2. Before putting the food in your mouth, look at it carefully. Notice how it looks—its color, its texture, its shape. Pay attention to how it smells.

3. Notice what's happening in your body, as well, and any physical sensations you are experiencing. Are you feeling hungry or full? Is saliva forming in your mouth?

4. As you take the food into your mouth, pay attention to the taste and sensation of the food on your tongue. How does the food feel in your mouth? What is the taste—sweet, sour, bitter, salty? As you chew slowly and swallow, what physical sensations do you feel?

5. If you notice your mind wandering, gently bring it back to the experience of eating. Notice any thoughts or feelings, but do not attach to or judge them—simply let them pass and refocus on eating.

6. Continue this practice throughout your meal, trying to be present with each bite of food. Treat each forkful as a new experience and continue to bring your mind back to this experience as it wanders.

7. Try to practice mindful eating with at least one snack or meal each day. With some practice, it will become more natural.

What do you think the benefits of practicing mindful eating may be for you, specifically? Think about how it may impact your procrastination and write your answers below:

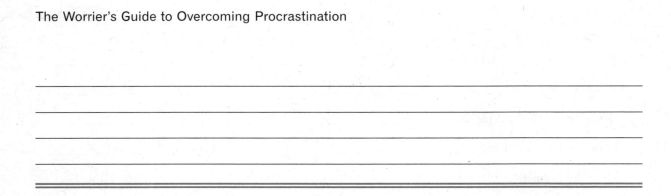

Now let's move on to mindfulness every day.

Step Three: Make Everyday Tasks Mindful

You can practice mindfulness by simply paying attention to activities you do every day. Most of us barely register everyday tasks like brushing our teeth, cooking our dinner, putting on our socks, or sitting in a chair. Yet each of these tasks generates an array of sensations and feelings that, though we may hardly notice, holds the key to becoming more present in our lives. Remember, noticing what is happening in your life *right now* is a skill that will help you not only to live each moment more fully but to prevent the anxiety and worry spirals that keep you stuck in the past or future.

EXERCISE: Mindfulness Today

1. First choose your task. Find an everyday task that you usually do automatically, without much thought. It could be anything, but some ideas are brushing your teeth, cooking dinner, putting on your socks, sitting in a chair, walking, washing your face, taking a shower, or driving to work.

2. For the next week, each time you do this task, do it mindfully. Pay attention with your whole body. Use each of your senses to notice the sensations that occur throughout the task—how things feel, smell, sound, look, and taste. Pay attention to things you would not usually notice. Immerse yourself in the moment as much as possible. Make your movements conscious and deliberate.

3. Gently redirect your attention as it begins to wane. Don't worry and don't judge your mind for wandering, simply bring it back to experience the task at hand.

Continue to practice awareness of daily tasks. Challenge yourself to make at least one routine task mindful each day, and keep track of your success using the chart below.

Mindfulness Practice Sheet

Day/Date	Task	Notes/Thoughts

Step Four: Watch Your Thoughts Pass Through

As you already know, our thoughts strongly impact the way we feel and the way we respond to situations. For anxious procrastinators, it may feel like the same thoughts play endlessly. *I'll never get it done. It won't be good enough. I can't do it right now.* Sometimes these thoughts become so familiar that you don't even notice them anymore. Yet there they are—a constant litany of worry and self-doubt—leading you to avoid, distract, and procrastinate. Mindfulness not only can help you become more aware of these thoughts, it can also help you disconnect from them. Remember, thoughts are only thoughts. They are temporary and fleeting. They are not real, they are not you, they do not define you. They are literally nothing. Let them pass through without judging. Use the following exercise to realize your thoughts for what they are: just thoughts and nothing more.

EXERCISE: Watch Your Thoughts

1. Sit comfortably in your chosen spot. Take a few deep breaths and, using your mindful breathing, pay attention to the sensations that your breathing creates.

2. Without judging, notice the thought you're having and simply label it as a thought. For instance, instead of *My presentation will be a flop*, it would be *I'm having the thought that my presentation will be a flop*. Rather than *I'm a complete failure*, it's *I'm having the thought that I'm a complete failure*.

3. Continue labeling your thoughts while you practice. If you find yourself judging your thoughts, remember to gently redirect your mind to just labeling them. Practice labeling your thoughts in this way for a few minutes.

4. Now watch these thoughts as they enter your mind and pass through, like clouds in the sky. Imagine each thought as a puffy white cloud rolling across the blue sky. They come into your mind and float through without stopping—like the clouds, you can't control how fast or slowly they move but can only watch them as they float past you.

5. Continue this practice for five minutes or as long as you feel comfortable. Just notice the thought as it enters your mind, label it as a thought, and watch it pass through on a cloud. Notice, label, watch it pass. Notice, label, watch it pass.

6. As you settle in and become more comfortable in the practice of labeling your thoughts and allowing them to move through your mind, try to move this strategy into your everyday life. Whenever you notice you're anxious, worried, or procrastinating, just notice the thought going through your mind and tag it for what it is—only a thought—and let it pass by.

Now, let's continue to work toward bringing mindfulness to your everyday experience.

Step Five: Center Yourself Throughout the Day

Now that you have practiced breathing, eating, and doing everyday tasks in a mindful way and watching your thoughts pass through, it's time to move this practice into your life more fully. Remember—you can be mindful anywhere, at any time. Practice centering yourself throughout your day. If you notice that you're anxious, avoiding, or procrastinating, use the steps below to refocus on the present moment.

EXERCISE: Getting Centered Anytime

1. Stop what you're doing and take a deep breath.

2. Using each of your senses, notice what you see, smell, hear, taste, and feel.

3. Look around and note three things that you can see.

4. What do you hear? Try to count at least three things.

5. Pay attention to three things you feel touching your skin.

6. Remember to include in your awareness what you smell and what you taste.

Use this exercise anytime you find you're worrying or anxious or just feel the need to center yourself. You may find that you use it many times each day to refocus on the present moment. Practice doing this now, using the spaces below to take notes on your experience.

Centering Practice

What I see:

1. _____

2. _____

3. _____

What I hear:

1. _____

2. _____

3. _____

What I feel:

1. _____

2. _____

3. _____

What I smell:

1. _____

2. _____

3. _____

What I taste:

1. _____

2. _____

3. _____

How did you do? Most people are surprised at how many things they notice when they focus. Though you don't need to take notes each time you refocus yourself throughout the day, you may find it helpful to do so the first few times you practice or when you feel particularly distracted or anxious. If you find that writing distracts you from the experience, of course you may skip that step. The more you practice refocusing yourself to the present moment, the more natural it will feel and the easier it will be to prevent your worry-avoidance spirals from developing.

TACKLE YOUR CONCERNS ABOUT MINDFULNESS

If you are like our clients, you probably have some questions and concerns about your practice of mindfulness. This is normal—being present in the moment is quite different from our usual way of interacting with our environment. It may feel awkward, insincere, or boring at first. It may take some time before you see the benefits of mindfulness on your anxiety, and perhaps even longer before you see it improving your procrastination and avoidance. This can be frustrating, and the temptation to give up can be strong. You aren't alone in your frustrations, but keep trying. It takes time to break a longstanding habit, but the benefits of doing so will be worth it. Below are some common comments we hear from our clients about the practice of mindfulness—see if any of your concerns are echoed here.

Mindfulness Takes Too Much Time

It's true that being mindful takes us out of the hustle and bustle of our lives. When you're harried by deadlines, taking even a few minutes away from the task at hand seems impossible. However, consider that you are reading this book because you're already losing time to worry, anxiety, and procrastination. Spending some time now to practice being present in the moment and breaking this cycle will pay off in the long run by decreasing the time you spend anxious and avoiding.

I'm Not Doing It Right

You may feel like your mind is wandering all over the place, and that you're just no good at this mindfulness thing. It's natural to want to get this right, but recall that it is only human for your mind to wander at times. Don't be overly harsh with yourself or judge the experience—simply keep refocusing when you notice that your attention wanes. The success is in continued practice and perseverance in redirecting your attention to the present moment, not in never needing to redirect it. Consider it an opportunity to practice refocusing whenever you notice your thoughts stray.

Being Mindful Makes Me More Anxious

Being aware of your emotions can sometimes make them seem more intense. While they may actually be intensified, it's more likely that you are just more aware of your anxiety and that sitting with it is initially quite uncomfortable. But we already know that avoiding or trying to distract yourself from anxiety doesn't work well and, if it works at all, it is only a temporary relief. Allow your anxiety to exist and to pass through without fighting it or attaching to it and you'll find that it loses its power.

I Procrastinate About Doing My Mindfulness Practice

Of course, it may be a challenge to practice when the very reason you're practicing is that you have a habit of procrastinating. But forget your track record and forget what may happen tomorrow, and just focus on being mindful in this moment. There will be obstacles and there will be setbacks—you don't need to be perfect. Just fit mindfulness into your life wherever you can and do your best.

NEXT STEPS

After you've practiced the steps in this chapter and find yourself more aware and more mindful of the present, continue to integrate this practice into your life when you can. If you notice you're anxious or procrastinating, bring yourself into the present moment. Use your mindfulness along with your other skills to diminish your anxiety and worry as you move on to the next section of this book and learn to confront your fears, set better goals, and manage time more effectively. If you are interested in more information about mindfulness or other ways to practice, you may try *Calming Your Anxious Mind: How Mindfulness and Compassion Can Free You from Anxiety, Fear, and Panic* (2007) by Jeffrey Brantley or *Wherever You Go, There You Are* (1994) by Jon Kabat-Zinn.

Key Points

◆ Anxiety is a vicious cycle, and being more aware or mindful of the present can break this spiral of worry and avoidance.

◆ Being mindful means staying in the present—paying attention on purpose to the moment you are in without judging it.

◆ Mindfulness-based therapies have been found to be very effective in decreasing anxiety.

◆ Practicing exercises like breathing or eating mindfully and being mindful in everyday tasks can help you become more present and decrease your anxiety.

◆ Labeling fears or worries for what they are—just thoughts—and learning to allow them to pass through your mind without judgment will help you to break the anxiety-procrastination cycle.

◆ You can integrate mindfulness into your daily life and use it to center yourself whenever you worry or find yourself anxious or procrastinating.

PART 3

Get Moving on Your Goals

Confront Your Fears

How many times have you heard, "You worry too much," or "Stop worrying about it, things will turn out fine"? If you're an anxious procrastinator, probably more times than you can count. In fact, this is exactly what most procrastinators are trying to do—stop worrying, stop thinking about it, stop feeling so anxious. So they distract themselves from, avoid, and put off the tasks behind the anxiety, trying to think about anything else. On the surface, it can seem like good common sense; if something is worrying you, then stop thinking about it, and if you don't like doing it, then don't do it. It seems like it should work. So why doesn't it?

THE AVOIDANCE TRAP

It would certainly be easier if avoidance did the trick—we'd just watch the football game, clean the kitchen, and forget about that looming deadline. But, unfortunately, avoidance doesn't work—if it did, no one would be reading this book. As a procrastinator, you already know better than anyone that putting things off and trying to put them out of your mind doesn't help. It doesn't make the task or decision go away, it doesn't accomplish anything, and it doesn't make you feel any less anxious, because you can never really forget about what you're supposed to be doing or what you should be deciding. In fact, trying *not* to think about it can backfire and lead you to think about it even more. Take a minute to try this experiment that we often use with our clients to help them understand the futility of trying to suppress anxious thoughts.

EXERCISE: Don't Think of a Red Balloon

Find an egg timer or a watch with an alarm and set it for one minute. Or, if you prefer, find a partner to time you. Close your eyes and think about whatever you'd like. But no matter what, do *not* think of a red balloon. Don't think of the word "balloon," and certainly don't allow an image of a balloon to come into your mind! Stick with it for a full minute and count how many times you slip up and allow thoughts or images of the balloon to enter your mind.

How did you do? If you're like most of us, you probably weren't very successful at all. Did you notice that the more you tried to not think about it, the more the balloon popped into your mind? Some scientific studies have found the same thing: the more we try to suppress thoughts, the more likely they are to occur (Wegman 1994). And even when people are successful, they find it very difficult to maintain this level of concentration for very long. It's exhausting! For a procrastinator, this avoidance tactic feeds into the never-ending worry-avoidance cycle. It keeps you scrambling to find things to distract from your worry about impending deadlines but never really sets you free from the anxiety or allows you to enjoy these distractions.

Say, though, that you could manage to not think about what worries you. That wouldn't help either, because avoiding the thoughts that cause you discomfort may actually increase your fears in the long run. By avoiding thoughts that upset you, you validate them as a real threat or danger and set yourself up to avoid more in the future. Avoidance undermines your confidence in your ability to tolerate these thoughts, to manage your anxiety, and to face tasks. As a result, avoidance makes the fear even more powerful. Avoiding your worries by delaying these tasks keeps you from learning that you really could face them and that nothing horrible would happen if you did.

As you learned in chapter 4, one of the most effective ways for you to conquer your fear is simply to face it. Of course, directly confronting feared situations, thoughts, or images is a simple idea, but—as you know—it's not easy. You used exposure therapy in chapter 4 to practice confronting situations related to your fears of failure and success, and you can use it in the same way now to learn to comfortably face *any* fears or worries you have that contribute to your procrastination.

Most people can see that avoiding the tasks or decisions they've been putting off is not the best path to building confidence and productivity, but they are skeptical when they hear that a good way to have fewer worries is to actually worry *more* on purpose. But it's true—cognitive behavioral treatment that includes exposure to worrisome thoughts and images has been found by some researchers to produce significant decreases in anxiety and worry (Ladouceur et al. 2000).

Habituation to Worry

How can intentionally worrying more lead to less worry? Good question. Frequently, our patients raise the objection that they already worry constantly and it doesn't seem to help. However, the difference is that when people worry spontaneously they rarely settle on one worry at a time. Worries tend to shift quickly from one to the next in a process called *chaining*. It usually happens so fast that there's barely time for individual worries to be noticed, let alone objectively evaluated (Zinbarg, Craske, and Barlow 1993), and the result is escalation of anxiety with each successive thought.

Think about the last time you worried about a task you were putting off—your taxes, a project at work or school, cleaning the garage. Chances are that the thoughts you had came fast and furious. *I don't know where to start. I'll never get it done. It will turn out horribly. I can't do it. It's too much for me to handle.* And it works the same way with decisions as well—finding a gym, choosing a day care, picking a dentist. *Which one should I choose? What if I'm wrong? What if there are better options? How will I know for sure? Maybe I'll regret it.* And on and on until you got so overwhelmed that you didn't do or decide anything at all.

During intentional worry exposure, you stick with one thought at a time. In doing this, you'll find that the longer you stay with and focus on that thought, the less it bothers you. The process of habituation works with situations, as you found with your practice in chapter 4, as well as with anxious thoughts. Research finds that by sticking with the thought that scares you, your anxiety will decrease over time (Foa and Kozak 1986). Distracting yourself from a thought or avoiding a particular worry will interfere with the process of habituation and thus maintain the anxiety that you feel. By learning to focus on one worry at a time, by worrying about it on purpose, and by sticking with the worry rather than distracting yourself, you will lower your anxiety in response to that thought and find yourself better able to complete the task you've been avoiding.

HOW TO USE EXPOSURE TO CONQUER ANXIOUS PROCRASTINATION

Now that you know the secret behind worry exposure—habituation to the thoughts you fear—you're ready to learn three key steps to using it to conquer your anxiety and procrastination. These steps are:

1. Developing your exposure hierarchy

2. Choosing the most effective method of exposure

3. Practicing exposure until you habituate

Step One: Develop Your Exposure Hierarchy

The idea of confronting your fears about the very situations you've been avoiding may sound scary. But remember, you will be facing these fears *gradually*, starting with the things that bother you least and working up to the hardest. The practice you get with these initial exposures will help you to deal with your bigger fears more easily.

Start by thinking about anxiety on a scale of 0 to 100. An anxiety level of 100 would mean the most distressing thought, image, or worry you can imagine, while 0 would indicate no anxiety at all. The midpoint of 50 would represent a moderate level of anxiety or distress, something that's challenging but still relatively tolerable. When estimating your anxiety level, keep in mind that you are guessing at the discomfort you would feel if you were exposed to this worry, thought, or image and you did *not* avoid or engage in any distraction or avoidance behaviors. Try to come up with a range of items from low to high anxiety and aim for at least ten items on your exposure hierarchy, but don't worry if you have more or fewer.

As an example, Grace's exposure list is below. Grace procrastinated on going to the doctor because she worried that he would scold her for being overweight or would find something seriously wrong with her health. She put off making the appointment until she was "in better shape," but, as a result, it had been many years since her last physical, her weight continued to climb, and she felt increasingly anxious about her health. Her goal was to feel more comfortable scheduling and attending the physical with her doctor by exposing herself to the thoughts, images, and worries that fed her anxiety.

Grace's Exposure List

Anxious Thought, Image, or Worry	Anxiety
Imagining the doctor telling me I have a serious illness	*100*
Seeing myself waiting in the exam room for the doctor	*90*
Looking at informational pamphlets on diseases or illnesses	*85*
Thinking, "He will tell me I'm too fat and have to lose weight"	*80*
Imagining being weighed in by the nurse	*70*
"What if I have cancer or heart disease?"	*65*
Reading information on nutrition and healthy BMI	*55*
"They'll wonder why I haven't been there in so long"	*40*

Notice that Grace rated her anxiety in response to the worries she has about going to the doctor and imagined thoughts about the situation, as well as anticipated anxiety in actual activities that reminded her of the situation, like reading information about nutrition. Now you give it a try. You may find it easiest to start with two anchor points. Think of a situation that you have been avoiding and that would cause you a great deal of distress to confront. Then consider the thoughts, images, or worries you have about that situation. Choose the one that causes you the most anxiety, and you can make that the top item on your hierarchy, a 100. Next, take one of the thoughts that would cause you only a moderate degree of anxiety to face and make that your midpoint, 50. Now list your remaining worries, thoughts, and images based on whether they would be easier or harder to confront than your anchor items. If there are actual situations that trigger your worries, as reading information on nutrition or illnesses did for Grace, you can include those as well.

Exposure List

Anxious Thought, Image, or Worry	Anxiety

Step Two: Choose Your Exposure Method

While there are many types of exposure, there are two in particular that are helpful in overcoming anxious procrastination. More than likely, you will need to use a combination of the two to address both your fearful thoughts and worries as well as any situations that trigger these worries. The two types are:

1. **In Vivo Exposure.** *In vivo exposures*, or real-life exposures, involve entering into situations that you fear. This may mean things like speaking in front of others, going to class, or shopping for new clothes. Your own fears will determine what in vivo exposures are appropriate for you.

2. **Imaginal Exposure.** When dealing with thoughts, worries, or images, you would use *imaginal exposure* instead. As the name suggests, an imaginal exposure is one using your imagination. To do an imaginal exposure, you can write out, record, and repeatedly listen to your feared worst-case scenario until anxiety comes down. This may include things like imagining negative feedback from your boss, failing an exam, or making the wrong decision.

Grace used both in vivo and imaginal exposure to address the items on her hierarchy. For instance, she practiced by repeatedly reading nutritional pamphlets and informational handouts on cardiac disease until she felt less anxious (in vivo exposure). She also created and imagined stories about the receptionists asking her why she hadn't been in for so long and about the nurse weighing her (imaginal exposure). Her imaginal exposure about her fear of the doctor telling her she needed to lose weight went like this:

It's cold in the room where I'm waiting for the doctor. I can hear the faint sound of his voice in the hallway or in the room next door, I can't really tell. I feel so self-conscious in this flimsy gown, and, as I look down at my shoes on the floor, I think for a second of just leaving. Maybe I could sneak out without anyone seeing me. But I don't even have time to finish that thought when there's a knock on the door. In comes Dr. Perry, looking pleasant enough. But I know that underneath that smile he is disappointed in me. He reviews the notes the nurse has written, and then his smile disappears. He looks at me grimly and says, "Grace, you've gained twenty-five pounds since your last visit. With your family history, that's unacceptable. You need to go on a strict regimen of diet and exercise immediately or I'm afraid you will not live very long. I'm setting up an appointment for you to see the nutritionist right away." I know he's right, but the disapproving tone of his voice makes my stomach turn. I'm so embarrassed I want to disappear.

After writing out this scene, Grace recorded it on audiotape and, while listening, imagined it as vividly as possible. She had difficulty hearing this story at first and often felt the urge to distract herself or turn it off. But she did her best to concentrate on the scenario as if it were actually happening and kept with it for twenty to thirty minutes each time she practiced. She found that the more she listened, the easier it got and the lower her anxiety became. Eventually the story didn't make her very anxious at all, and she felt ready to make her appointment for a physical. When Dr. Perry did talk to her about her weight, Grace was much less anxious than she imagined she would be, feeling less like escaping and more prepared to handle it.

Step Three: Practice Exposure

Now that you've created your hierarchy and know about the different types of exposure, the next step is to practice. You can use the following guidelines when planning your exposure practices. Begin by selecting an item low on your hierarchy—it should be something challenging but not overwhelming. Practice exposing yourself to that situation, thought, or worry until your anxiety diminishes by at least half. So, if you start out with an exposure that you've rated as a 40 on your anxiety scale, you should try to focus on the exposure, without distracting yourself, until your anxiety decreases to about a 20. Anxiety should come down from its peak during each exposure exercise. You should also notice that your anxiety may start out or peak a bit lower each time you practice. Stay with the item until it causes you only mild or no anxiety and then move up to the next item on your hierarchy and repeat the process.

Everyone responds differently, so it may take you only a few days of practice with an item before you move on, or it may take a week or longer. Continue to confront your fears until you have completed all the items on your hierarchy. You can use the form below to record your anxiety during each exposure practice and to track your progress over time.

Exposure Practice Form

Date: _____

Start Time: _____   End Time: _____

Anxiety Level (0–100):

Start: _____   *Notes:*

10 minutes: _____   _____

20 minutes: _____   _____

30 minutes: _____   _____

40 minutes: _____   _____

50 minutes: _____   _____

60 minutes: _____   _____

End: _____

WHAT TO EXPECT DURING EXPOSURE

The overall effect of exposure will be a decrease in anxiety, but you may find that initially your anxiety is higher than normal. This is expected and, in fact, your anxiety *needs* to be of at least moderate intensity during the exposure period in order for the exercise to be effective. By the end of each designated exposure time, though, you should see some reduction in your anxiety from its maximum level that day. As you repeat the same exposure, you should see a decrease in your initial anxiety ratings from day to day. Some people also find that their anxiety tends to decrease faster the more times they repeat the exercise. Remember, you're building your endurance and working hard to increase your tolerance of these thoughts and situations, so it's normal to feel physically tired or mentally fatigued. As you confront your fears, expect to feel temporarily more anxious; but if you stick with it, you should soon start to see positive results and reduced anxiety.

WHAT TO DO AFTER EXPOSURE

During an exposure, it's crucial for you to feel the anxiety and to not do anything to distract from that experience. Allowing the anxiety to subside on its own is a critical requirement for successful exposure therapy. Be sure to refrain from reassuring yourself or talking yourself out of the fear until *after* the twenty to thirty minutes of exposure time has elapsed. Remember, the anxiety will decrease on its own. After the exposure, however, you may find it helpful to use the skills you learned earlier in this book to challenge your fearful thoughts. You could identify any cognitive distortions in your thinking, generate evidence against the worry thought, or use your mindfulness skills to refocus yourself. By waiting until after the exposure you will learn that your anxiety does diminish on its own, but you will also get good practice at using your other skills.

HOW MUCH EXPOSURE TO DO

While exposure can be a helpful tool in overcoming your procrastination by helping you to worry less and face situations you fear, too much exposure can become its own delay tactic. There is no exact answer for how much exposure is the right amount. It is up to you to be aware of how you are using this valuable tool. Be sure to move up your hierarchy as soon as an item stops causing you anxiety, even if you dread the next step. Be wary of practicing too many imaginal exposures on your hierarchy but never getting to the situation that you fear. Be consistent in your practice, and don't drag out each exposure by doing it only infrequently. Remember that you don't have to include *every* worry, thought, image, or situation you fear on your hierarchy. In confronting some fears, you should notice that practice will generalize to others as well. If you're having difficulty with exposure or if you find that your anxiety doesn't seem to be decreasing, the following strategies may help.

Tips for Successful Exposure

- Practice your exposure daily. Doing it sporadically won't work, and you will likely maintain the same high levels of anxiety. Make your efforts count!

- Be sure to stick with it. People are sometimes tempted to quit the exposure early because experiencing anxiety can be unpleasant. Often they discontinue the exercise right at the peak level of anxiety, just before it's about to subside. It only *feels* like the anxiety will never end. Hang in there—it will go down with time.

- If you are using imaginal exposure, make your scenario as vivid and as specific as possible. Include details about the sounds, smells, sights, thoughts, and feelings involved. Write the scenario in the first person and in the present tense, as if it were actually happening to you right now. Be sure to focus on just one worry at a time.

- Be sure to use your hierarchy to determine how to pace your exposures. Always pick something that is challenging but not overwhelming. When an exposure becomes easy, move up your hierarchy to the next one.

◆ Be sure to wait until *after* the twenty to thirty minutes of exposure time has elapsed before challenging any cognitive distortions. Don't reassure yourself during the exposure or try to talk yourself out of the fear.

◆ If you notice that your anxiety doesn't decrease, look closely for any subtle avoidance, distraction, or other behaviors that you may be engaging in. It can be reflexive to use these types of coping strategies, but they work only in the short term. In the long run, they end up maintaining your anxiety.

Exposure therapy can seem a little daunting at first, but by keeping at it and working through your fear, you'll gain more control over your anxiety and your tendency to procrastinate.

NEXT STEPS

Now that you have some practice confronting your worries, anxious thoughts, and images, how do you feel? If you feel less worried and more ready to tackle the tasks you've been putting off, good for you! If you're having trouble, take a look back at the steps and give them another try. Did you have trouble finding time to practice? If so, you may find the upcoming chapters helpful in prioritizing this exercise and making time to do it.

Key Points

◆ Avoiding fears by trying not to think about them can actually result in increased worry and anxiety.

◆ Sticking with worries about a feared situation long enough results in a decrease of anxiety, or habituation.

◆ Two kinds of exposure, in vivo and imaginal, can be helpful for anxious procrastinators.

◆ By systematically confronting your fears in a step-by-step manner, you can become more comfortable with your anxious thoughts, images, and worries and decrease your avoidance of feared situations.

9

Set Effective Goals

At the beginning of each therapy session, we ask our patients the same thing: "What would you like to work on in today's session?" As you can imagine, over the years we've heard a wide variety of answers. Some of our clients are unsure. They know they feel anxious and want to feel better, but they lack an exact idea of what they want to accomplish in each meeting. Others look to us, asking us what we think might be best to focus on. Some seem surprised by the question, taken aback a bit by the notion that effective goals are an important part of therapy. The patients that tend to make the fastest and best progress are those who answer our question with a clear, specific goal in mind. Elaine, for instance, answered this question quite clearly: "I get anxious around my sister-in-law. She intimidates me. I'd like to learn new ways of interacting with her so our relationship can be more comfortable for me." As you can see, this is a clear, specific goal and will help Elaine to make progress in therapy.

It can be difficult to set good goals, but doing so is a crucial step in overcoming anxious procrastination. In this chapter, you'll learn how to set solid, attainable goals and then accomplish them. You'll learn how to break down broader values into well-defined, short-term step-by-step goals. You also learn the difference between ineffective and effective goals.

WHY IS EFFECTIVE GOAL SETTING SO IMPORTANT?

Learning to set goals is crucial to overcoming anxious procrastination. As someone who procrastinates out of worry and anxiety, you may have difficulty setting goals. You may find that you struggle with defining exactly what you want to accomplish on a day-to-day basis. You might also struggle with setting larger, longer-term goals. When you do have free time, maybe you're not sure what to do with it. As a result, it often gets wasted, and at the end of the day, you feel little sense of accomplishment.

By setting clear and effective goals, you'll find that you can regulate your thoughts and behaviors to achieve what you want. Goals serve the essential role of orienting our actions to help us progress in life.

In addition, we find once our clients learn the steps to setting effective goals, they often report numerous benefits. Their mood improves, they feel more confident and less stressed, and procrastination diminishes. Our patients report a sense of energy and vitality as meaning and purpose return to their lives. They experience the joy of accomplishing their goals and the thrill of feeling as though their life is progressing, not mired in indecision and lack of direction.

In the next section, we'll show you a five-step plan to setting effective goals. You'll learn to ditch the bad habit of having vague, ineffective goals—or worse yet, no goals—and replace it with clear, specific goals that move you rapidly toward the life you want to live.

HOW TO SET GOOD GOALS

Now that you understand the importance of goal setting, you're ready to learn how to set good ones. You can attain this skill by using our five-step plan for effective goal setting. By improving your goal-setting skills, you'll be more effective and can reduce anxious procrastination in your life.

The five steps of effective goal setting are:

1. Determining your values

2. Setting a goal

3. Identifying the steps to achieve it

4. Anticipating problems

5. Rewarding yourself

Let's take a look at these steps in more detail. We'll go through each of them and offer several exercises along the way.

Step One: Determine Your Values

Before you determine your values, let's define the term. What exactly is a value? *Values* can be defined as chosen life directions (Hayes 2005). They are decisions we make about the broader issues in life that put us on a specific path. Values help us organize our choices and behaviors; they lead us to follow a certain direction, make certain choices, and choose certain goals. Without values, we'd be overwhelmed by life's choices. We'd be foundering in a sea of too many options. The values we choose, consciously or unconsciously, guide us to set goals and make decisions that move us toward those values.

Certainly values shift over the course of our lives. What's important to us at age twenty is often very different from what's important to us at sixty. Judy was fifty when she came to therapy for anxiety. She had seen her mother, who was eighty, outlive her money. Her mom often had to borrow money from Judy. Judy, a free spender, always placed high value on material goods. She saw her values impacted by the fear of becoming like her mother. Suddenly, driving a fancy car seemed less important than saving for her older years. This reflected a shift in Judy's values. Based on this change, Judy set new goals for herself that involved saving for her future as well as cutting back on her current expenses.

If you suffer from anxious procrastination, it can be enormously helpful to spend some time considering your values. It's these values that give structure to your day-to-day life. If you are unclear on your values, you may find yourself paralyzed by options. You might find this especially true with your free time, such as the evenings or weekends. During those times, you may find yourself conflicted with various possibilities, and you might cope with feeling overwhelmed by simply doing nothing. Clarifying your values can help resolve these conflicts and give you a sense of direction, meaning, and purpose.

Let's take a look at some examples of values:

- Health

- Relationships

- Spirituality

- Family

- Parenting

- Money

- Friends

- Career

- Material goods

- Altruism

- Education

- Recreation

- Other: _____

EXERCISE: What Are Your Values?

Now take some time to reflect on this list. What is most important to you? Which values strike you as particularly crucial at this point in your life? List the five things that are most important to you (in descending order) below.

1. _____

2. _____

3. _____

4. _____

5. _____

Jim is a thirty-nine-year-old entrepreneur who has struggled with anxiety and avoidance for much of his life. As attempt after attempt at controlling his procrastination failed, it became clear that Jim lacked a core set of values with which to guide his efforts. When Jim took inventory of his values, he came up with the following list of values that he felt were most important to him:

1. Health

2. Family

3. Career

4. Friends

5. Religion

Jim was surprised at the outcome of this exercise. After reviewing his values, it was clear he wasn't spending enough time or effort on his top priorities. He realized that his past attempts at productivity had failed because he was focusing on the wrong things—things that weren't important to him. Jim realized he needed to change and decided to set some clear, specific goals that would help him live more in line with his values.

Step Two: Set a Goal

Our goals align us with our values. If we set our goals appropriately, they will move us along on a path to living a life that fulfills our values. But a goal is also quite different from a value. While our values represent the things that are most important to us, a *goal* is a concrete and achievable task (Hayes 2005). Goals also determine our actions. They drive how hard we'll work at something and for how long (Locke 2002).

Problems with procrastination can occur at both the value and the goal level. If you're stuck at the value level, you'll feel overwhelmed by indecision, unable to choose a path. If you struggle at the goal level, you'll know where you want to go—you just won't know how to most effectively get there. When considering creating goals that line up with your values, it's crucial to know the keys to setting good goals.

EFFECTIVE GOALS

Edwin A. Locke is one of the foremost researchers on goal setting. He's spent his career researching what constitutes an effective goal and what makes for an ineffective goal. The guidelines for effective goal setting in this chapter are based on his work (Locke 2002). In researching effective goals, he found that good goals require:

- *Difficulty:* This characteristic might seem counterintuitive. You might think that setting a small, easy goal is the way to go. Research proves otherwise (Locke 2002). It seems that the more difficult the goal, the more likely we are to work hard in order to meet it. Falling short on a difficult goal means that you've still accomplished a lot. Consider golfer Tiger Woods. In his sport, most golfers set the goal of winning a tournament. Tiger's career goal is to break Jack Nicklaus's record by winning nineteen major championships. By setting this difficult goal, Tiger has worked harder and produced more than most other golfers in history.

- *Specificity:* The clearer and more specific the goal, the better. Often, numbers are helpful when setting a specific goal. For example, "lose twenty pounds" is a more specific—and therefore better—goal than "lose weight."

- *Feedback*: The ability to track your progress is another key to effective goal setting. Feedback allows you to be aware of your performance and to adjust your efforts accordingly. Feedback often goes hand in hand with being specific with your goals. For example, if you set the goal to lose twenty pounds, a scale would provide you with clear performance feedback. This information is essential to continued progress. It provides us with key information about our performance as we work toward our goals.

- *Commitment:* Making a commitment is crucial to success in achieving goals. Therefore, setting goals that you are committed to is essential. That's what makes clarifying your values so important. Those values help you choose goals that you are committed to—goals that are *important* to you.

- *Achievability:* The final key to setting a good goal is to select a goal that is within your capabilities. An effective goal is one that you believe you can meet. Difficult goals are useful in enhancing performance and overcoming procrastination. However, the goal should be something you generally have the abilities to reach.

Examples of effective goals include:

- Lose twenty pounds.

- Save $1,000 by the end of the year.

- Lower my cholesterol by twenty points.

- Attend church every Sunday.

- Have dinner as a family five days per week.

INEFFECTIVE GOALS

As you might imagine, ineffective goals are mainly the opposite of effective goals. We set these goals with good intentions, but they don't lead us efficiently toward our values. Instead, we get mired in the goals themselves.

Examples of ineffective goals include:

◆ Improve my health.

◆ Get along better with my family.

◆ Be happier.

◆ Try my best.

◆ Enjoy life more.

◆ Stop procrastinating.

Following is a table to help you quickly assess whether the goals you've chosen will be effective for you.

Choosing Goals that Work

Effective Goals	Ineffective Goals
Challenging	Too easy
Specific	Vague
Measurable	Not measurable
Important to you	Unimportant to you
Matches your self-efficacy	Doesn't fit your self-efficacy

SHORT-TERM GOALS VS. LONG-TERM GOALS

Now that you're familiar with the keys to effective goal setting, you might also find it helpful to think in terms of short-term goals and long-term goals. *Short-term goals*, as the name suggests, are those that can be accomplished in the near future. They represent guideposts along the way. On our journey, they keep us oriented toward our destination. *Long-term goals* start to approach our values and take a longer time to reach. They represent a destination. Ideally, your short-term goals, long-term goals, and values work in concert with each other, each leading toward living a life that fulfills your highest values.

Let's look at an example of how values, short-term goals, and long-term goals fit together. April, a twenty-four-year-old, sought treatment for procrastination because she was having trouble finishing school. She had dropped out of several colleges, and at the time of treatment she wasn't enrolled at any school. She was avoiding completing the applications and submitting the necessary paperwork to start school again. In therapy, she looked at her values, long-term goals, and short-term goals. She identified her value and long-term and short-term goals like this:

◆ *Value*: Education

◆ *Long-Term Goal:* Get a college diploma

◆ *Short-Term Goal:* Submit an application to the local state school before the deadline

Once April clearly identified her value and her long-term and short-term goal, she was ready to move onto the next step and break her short-term goal down into more manageable steps.

EXERCISE: Practice Setting Goals

Now it's your turn to practice setting good goals. Take a look at the value hierarchy you created earlier. Choose one value from the list and write down a long-term and short-term goal related to that value in the spaces provided.

Value:

My long-term goal is: _____ .

My short-term goal is: _____ .

Now review your goals. Do they meet the criteria of an effective goal? Are they challenging? Specific? Can you get feedback? Are you committed to them? Are they within your capabilities to accomplish? If you answered no to any of these, consider revising your goals to ensure they meet all the criteria of effective goals.

Jim reviewed his value list and decided he needed to focus on his health. His initial goal was "Get healthier." Based on the criteria for effective goals, do you see any problems with Jim's goal? He clearly values health and is setting a goal accordingly. However, Jim's goal is simply too vague. Jim revised his goal to make it more specific. His new short-term goal became "Lower my cholesterol by thirty points." As you can see, this new goal is much more specific. It also meets the other criteria for effective goals. It's challenging, Jim is committed to it, he can get feedback along the way, and Jim feels it's a goal he has the know-how to accomplish.

Step Three: Identify the Steps to Achieve the Goal

Now that you've selected a long-term and a short-term goal that meet the effectiveness criteria, you're ready to break them down into smaller tasks. In this step, you'll choose your short-term goal and identify the smallest steps necessary to accomplish it. These steps represent mini-goals, the objectives that make up a short-term goal. The notion that each short-term goal is made up of several mini-goals and each long-term goal is made up of many short-term goals is captured in popular sayings such as "By the yard, life is hard. By the inch, life is a cinch." The strategy of mini-goals works particularly well not only when bigger goals can be paralyzing or overwhelming, but also when dealing with tasks that you avoid because they are boring, unpleasant, or scary.

For example, Sarah, a patient suffering from anxious procrastination, lived in downtown Chicago. At age twenty-four, she didn't have a driver's license; she had just never gotten around to it. However, after getting a new job in the suburbs as a pharmaceutical representative, she was suddenly faced with the need to drive to work each day. So she set a goal: "Get my driver's license." This is a short-term goal that worked in concert with Sarah's long-term goal of a career with this particular company and her values of financial success and rewarding work. The next step for her was to break down this short-term goal into individual steps. Her steps looked like this:

1. Apply for a learner's permit.

2. Find someone I can practice with.

3. Practice driving five hours a week.

4. Study the driver's ed book for thirty minutes a day.

5. Take the road test.

6. Get my license.

EXERCISE: Create Mini-goals

Take a look at the short-term goal you listed earlier. Now break it down into its smallest steps. These represent the mini-goals that it takes to reach your larger goal. List your steps below.

1. _____

2. _____

3. _____

4. _____

5. _____

As another example, we can look at Jim. After creating his goal of lowering his cholesterol by thirty points, his next task was to break this goal down into clear, specific steps. He thought of what he specifically needed to do to meet his goal. He came up with the following steps:

1. Run on the treadmill for thirty minutes, three times a week.

2. Eat three servings of oatmeal per day.

3. Eliminate red meat.

Jim felt that these three steps would help him live more in accordance with his value of being healthy and were the steps needed to achieve his goal of lowering his cholesterol by thirty points.

Step Four: Anticipate Problems

When you are identifying your values, choosing your goals, and selecting the steps necessary to meet your goals, you'll often feel a surge of energy and motivation. Like a horse chomping at the bit, you feel ready to take charge of your life and live in accordance with your values. The path is clearer now. You know what you want to do and how you want to do it. You feel vital, energized, and ready to take on life.

As great as that feeling of energy and enthusiasm is, you'll greatly increase the odds of your success if you complete the last two steps of the goal-setting process. In this next-to-last one, we turn our attention to the problems you might face as you work toward your goals. Once you start down the path to accomplishing your short-term and long-term goals, you'll find that bumps in the road are inevitable. A key step is asking yourself, "What could go wrong? What problems will I face as I work toward this goal?" Working in advance to find solutions to any possible problems can be enormously helpful.

EXERCISE: Identify Problems and Brainstorm Solutions

Go back and take a look at your short-term goal. Now think for a moment: What could possibly go wrong? What impediments to your progress might you face? On the form below, write every problem you can think of under the heading "Problem." Now, for each problem, brainstorm possible solutions. This way, you'll be prepared in advance for any snags that come your way.

Possible Solutions

Problem	Solution

Recall that Jim set a goal of lowering his cholesterol by thirty points. Once Jim broke down his goal step by step, he felt excited and energized. He had a clear path to meeting his goal. His next step was to identify any problems he might face and brainstorm possible solutions. He completed his sheet like this:

Jim's Possible Solutions

Problem	Solution
I run out of oatmeal.	*I know I need 21 servings per week. I can purchase a week's worth when I do my grocery shopping so I don't have to run back and forth to the store.*
I can't find the time to exercise.	*I can commit to a specific time each week: Monday, Wednesday, and Friday before work.*
My treadmill breaks.	*I can run outside, get a new treadmill, or join a gym.*
My knee hurts.	*I can do other forms of exercise that put less strain on my knee, such as swimming.*
I crave red meat too much.	*There are plenty of other foods I enjoy. I can reward myself with a cheeseburger when I reach my goal.*
I get bored with running on the treadmill.	*I could watch TV while on the treadmill, run outside, or switch to a different exercise for a while.*

Step Five: Plan to Reward Yourself

Setting goals and completing the steps required to achieve them is often hard work. It can be enormously helpful to see a light at the end of the tunnel. Planning to reward yourself when you achieve your goal gives you something to look forward to, some way to say "Nice job" after all your hard work. Completing a difficult goal that you value is often highly rewarding in itself. Nevertheless, good often comes from planning an external reward as well. Chapter 11 will help you to develop your reward system more fully, but for now take a moment to reflect on what you find enjoyable or pleasurable. Brainstorm and list your ideas below. It's okay to be bold and outlandish here. Be creative.

EXERCISE: Choose a Reward

My rewards could include:

1. _____

2. _____

3. _____

4. _____

5. _____

6. _____

7. _____

8. _____

9. _____

10. _____

Now choose one or more rewards from your list above.

When I achieve my goal, I will reward myself by: _____

NEXT STEPS

Now that you understand the keys to effective goal setting, you're ready to move on to the rest of this book. You'll take your new goal-setting skills into the upcoming chapters, where you'll learn how to manage your time better, communicate more assertively, and make changes to your environment on your path to overcoming anxious procrastination.

Key Points

◆ Learning to set effective goals is crucial to overcoming anxious procrastination. Once you set effective goals, you'll notice an increase in energy, productivity, and vitality.

◆ Effective goal setting consists of five key steps: determine your values, set a goal, identify the steps, anticipate problems, and reward yourself.

◆ Effective goals are challenging and specific and offer the possibility for feedback. Effective goals also involve a strong commitment on your part and a sense that you have the skills necessary to accomplish them.

◆ By implementing the five steps, you can dramatically improve your goal-setting skills. You'll find you become more productive, and your anxious procrastination will decrease as a result.

Manage Time More Effectively

Now that you better understand the fears behind your anxiety and how that worry leads to your procrastination, it's time to take the goals you set in the preceding chapter and make the time to work on them. The idea of time management is frightening and distasteful to many procrastinators, and it's easy to understand why—perhaps it brings to mind failed attempts at being productive, maybe it feels restrictive, artificial, or punitive, or maybe the idea brings up guilt over time lost already. Whatever the case, managing time better *is* a necessary step to procrastinating less. Boosted by the work you've already done to understand your fears and overcome the worry and anxiety that leads you to procrastinate, you may just find that this attempt at improving your time management skills is the one that finally works. Give it a try!

WHY LEARN TO MANAGE TIME BETTER?

The best reason to learn more effective time-management skills is that taking control of your schedule will have a positive impact on your worry. And if you worry less, you'll procrastinate less. But don't take our word for it—research studies have found that building time-management skills can decrease worry, avoidance, and procrastination (Van Eerde 2003). By creating a realistic and flexible plan for how you'll spend your time, you'll be less prone to making choices that are based in anxiety and less likely to choose ineffective paths to your goal. It makes sense—improving time management by better planning the course of your day can help you to prevent procrastination (Dietz, Hofer & Fries 2007).

And let's face it, procrastinators have a complicated relationship with time. The clock can become your adversary, mocking you as the seconds tick by in your game of chicken, while at the same moment it represents an endless fountain of possibility—a never-ending resource. Anxious procrastinators have a true love-hate relationship with time. They can vacillate wildly between underestimating and overestimating how much time is needed to complete a task. On one hand, it feels as though there is plenty of time to get things done, so why bother starting now when watching football, reading the newspaper, or talking on the phone are more appealing? On the other, it can seem like a project will take so much time that it becomes overwhelming—and since there isn't enough time right now to get this done anyway, it will have to wait until later. Time management is about more than just keeping a better calendar; it's about changing your relationship with time by becoming aware of your current habits, learning to accurately estimate time, and planning goals into your schedule. You'll learn that by stopping your tango with time, you can make it your ally instead.

PUTTING TIME MANAGEMENT INTO ACTION

In the same way that you learned to break down your goals in chapter 9, time-management skills can be broken down into a few simple steps. By learning each piece one at a time, you can tolerate the overwhelming task of managing time better and put it into action. There are four basic steps:

1. Developing awareness

2. Analyzing how you spend your time

3. Remembering your priorities

4. Planning your days (realistically!)

Step One: Develop Awareness

Many people who think they have a handle on where their time goes are actually unaware of the time they waste on unnecessary or unproductive tasks. Before you can improve how you spend your time, you first need to look at what you're doing with it now. For instance, Diane was a busy office manager who frequently felt harried and complained that there simply wasn't enough time in her day to complete all of her responsibilities. Her perception of her days at work was of rushing from meeting to meeting, putting out fires and fielding requests while important paperwork and required employee evaluations languished on her desk. As a result, she avoided her office because of the anxiety it created to see those missed deadlines piling up. Of course, this avoidance only put her farther behind. When asked to monitor her time, she agreed but asserted that it would be a useless endeavor, since she already knew the real problem was the unrealistic demands of her job, not the way she used her time. However, as Diane recorded her activities for a week, she was shocked. By monitoring, she was able to recognize how much time she spent performing tasks that could have been delegated to others, how frequent interruptions by others slowed her progress, and how she wasted valuable bits of time by answering personal e-mail at work or browsing the Internet. Noticing these things allowed Diane to restructure her schedule in a way that maximized her productivity, decreased her anxiety, and improved her job satisfaction.

For the next week, follow Diane's example and monitor your activities using the form below. Be sure to make copies first so you can use it for later exercises as well. Or, if you prefer, you can purchase a daily appointment calendar or use a notebook to create your own. This step is important, since it will give you a detailed idea of where you spend your time and what adjustments might help. Be sure to keep track of how much time you spend sleeping, eating, commuting, watching television, and running errands. Be as detailed as possible. Keep this form or your notebook or calendar with you and record activities as soon as you complete them. Don't rely on your memory or wait until the end of the day to fill out the form. For this exercise to be useful, you need an accurate picture of your schedule.

COMMON OBSTACLES TO MONITORING TIME

As you contemplate beginning your time-monitoring project, some negative thoughts may crop up. Let's take a look at some of the most common.

I already know how I spend my time. If, like Diane, you feel you don't need to do any monitoring because you already know how you spend your time, do the following simple experiment. Write down your estimates of how much time you spend in a day doing the activities we listed before (sleeping, eating, commuting, watching television, and running errands). Then monitor your time tomorrow—just for one day—to see how close your guesses were. Our patients usually find they weren't very accurate in their estimates. In fact, they're often quite surprised at the amount of time they spend on things like commuting or watching TV.

I'm too busy for this. Does keeping such close track of your schedule sound overwhelming to you? Do you feel like you don't have the time to do it? Keep in mind, this is only temporary. You don't have to do this exercise for the rest of your life—just one week. And by spending the time now, you'll gain more time in the future. Consider it an investment in decreasing your worry, anxiety, and stress and as the first step toward gaining more control over how you use your time.

I'll just put off doing this the way I put off other tasks. If you find yourself procrastinating on this exercise, pay attention to the thoughts that arise when you attempt to monitor your time. Do you worry that this try will fail like other attempts? Are you waiting to find the perfect calendar to start your monitoring? Do you doubt your ability to change? Use the strategies you learned in part 2 of this book to work through the fears that are holding you back, and remember that you are now armed with new skills to help you succeed.

Weekly Time-Management Form

Time	Monday	Tuesday	Wednesday	Thursday	Friday	Saturday	Sunday
6:00 am							
6:30 am							
7:00 am							
7:30 am							
8:00 am							
8:30 am							
9:00 am							
9:30 am							
10:00 am							
10:30 am							
11:00 am							
11:30 am							
12:00 pm							
12:30 pm							
1:00 pm							
1:30 pm							

Time	Monday	Tuesday	Wednesday	Thursday	Friday	Saturday	Sunday
2:00 pm							
2:30 pm							
3:00 pm							
3:30 pm							
4:00 pm							
4:30 pm							
5:00 pm							
5:30 pm							
6:00 pm							
6:30 pm							
7:00 pm							
7:30 pm							
8:00 pm							
8:30 pm							
9:00 pm							
9:30 pm							
10:00 pm							

Time	Monday	Tuesday	Wednesday	Thursday	Friday	Saturday	Sunday
10:30 pm							
11:00 pm							
11:30 pm							
12:00 am							
12:30 am							
1:00 am							
1:30 am							
2:00 am							
2:30 am							
3:00 am							
3:30 am							
4:00 am							
4:30 am							
5:00 am							
5:30 am							

Step Two: Analyze How You Spend Your Time

Did you record your activities for the week? If not, do so before you move on. It's an essential step in managing your time better. By recording your activities, you can look at where your time went so you know where to make adjustments. Once you've recorded your activities, analyze how you spent your time using the following steps:

1. Look at the activities you recorded over the past week. Can you group them into categories using the form below? Some possible categories include sleeping, eating, caring for your children, working, reading, watching TV, browsing the Internet, running errands, making phone calls, personal grooming or hygiene, cooking meals, doing household chores, commuting, and recreation. Use the categories on the form as a start, but add anything to the list that fits for you.

Grouping Your Categories

Categories	Time Spent
Sleeping	
Eating	
Child care	
Working	
Household chores	
Running errands	
Phone calls	
Grooming	
Cooking meals	
Commuting	
Recreation	
Other:	
Total Time Spent:	**168 hours**

2. Now, on the right side of that page, tally up how much time you spent over the past week doing activities in each category. Be sure that you account for all the hours in a week: 168.

3. Were you surprised by anything? Did you spend more time on anything than you thought you would? Was there anything you wish you'd done more of? How about less of? Did you spend any time doing unnecessary tasks? Anything that you wanted to get done but didn't? Record your answers here:

Wish I'd done more:

_____

_____

_____

_____

_____

Wish I'd done less:

_____

_____

_____

_____

_____

Step Three: Consider Your Priorities

In chapter 9, we asked you to prioritize your personal values. Now that you've had an opportunity to take a look at how you spend your time, ask yourself how closely the time you spent matches with those values. Of course, we can't always spend our time exactly the way we'd like—there is work to be done and bills to be paid. However, if you found yourself engaging in a lot of activities that were neither productive *nor* enjoyable, consider that in planning your upcoming week. If, like most anxious procrastinators, you found that you spent a lot of time in activities that were unnecessary while other important tasks went undone, the following strategy might help.

First, make a master list of things you want to accomplish this week. Include the goals you identified in the last chapter. Don't spend too much time on this step or worry if it isn't perfect—you can always add to this list as new goals or obligations arise. Then think about each task on your list and whether it falls into one of the following categories:

◆ **High Priority:** Extremely important and critical to complete this week

◆ **Medium Priority:** Very important, but not urgent that it be done this week

◆ **Low Priority:** Important and needs to be done, but not right away

Steve was head of the English department at the high school where he worked. His wife, a busy attorney, frequently became frustrated with him because he would bring work home every evening and, as a result, he spent little time with her or with his three young children. On weekends, Steve would hole himself up in the den grading papers or writing lesson plans, recommendation letters, or staff evaluations—usually well past deadline. Though Steve had a planning period at school, he rarely accomplished anything there, often telling himself that it wasn't enough time to get any real work done or that he'd just be interrupted anyway. Unbeknownst to his wife, his time in the den on weekends was also pretty unproductive—mostly spent worrying over what to do first, how he would explain missing his deadlines, and what his students and colleagues would think of him. His wife's frustration finally prompted Steve to reconsider his strategies. He used the values he identified—family, health, work—to guide his goals and to prioritize his weekly task list.

Steve's Tasks This Week

Weekly Master Task List	Priority Category (High, Medium, Low)
Spend 1 hour each night with family	*High*
Write recommendation letter due next week	*Medium*
Observe new English I class	*Medium*
Make phone call to friend	*Low*
~~*Research workshops for standardized testing*~~	~~*Low*~~
Exercise 2–3 times per week	*High*
Grocery shop	*Medium*
Take daughter to her soccer game on Saturday	*High*
Use planning hour to grade papers	*High*
Give feedback on staff syllabi	*Medium*
~~*Create study guide for the class*~~	~~*Low*~~
Review AP curriculum	*Low*
Revise budget	*Low*

As you can see, Steve created his task list to match not only the activities that had firm deadlines that week but also those that were most in line with his values. He made time for his family and his health and for those work activities that had impending deadlines. He was careful to be realistic in what he could accomplish and to be mindful of not designating too many activities as high priority when, in fact, they could wait. He deleted low-priority items when possible. For example, notice that he crossed off "Create study guide for class" and "Research workshops for standardized testing" from his list. After considering it, he decided that he could delegate these tasks to his teaching assistant, who would likely do a fine job and be happy to gain the experience.

Now you try it. Create your list of tasks for this week and prioritize them based on deadlines as well as how closely they match your values. If any project on your list is too big or overwhelms you, consider whether it could be broken down into smaller steps. If any tasks don't fit into one of these categories—if they are unimportant or unnecessary—cross them off your list altogether. Remember to also consider deleting the low-priority items from your list.

Tasks This Week

Weekly Master Task List	Priority Category (High, Medium, Low)

Step Four: Realistically Plan Your Days

Now look at your schedule for the week and write in any scheduled appointments, meetings, or other commitments that have a firm beginning and ending time. If these require travel, be sure to block off time for that too. Don't forget to include necessary activities like eating and sleeping! Next, take high-priority items from your master list and put them into the free slots in your schedule. There shouldn't be too many high-priority items—if it seems you have a lot (more than two or three each day), consider whether you are exaggerating their importance and the urgency that they get done right away. If any free time remains, take medium-priority tasks from the list and schedule them. Consider crossing off low-priority tasks, and schedule them only if time remains after you've accounted for high- and medium-priority tasks.

Remember to be flexible and to be realistic about what you can accomplish. Be sure also to leave some time on your schedule unaccounted for. Use this time for things that come up unexpectedly or to just have some downtime for yourself. Scheduling every minute of your day, being unrealistic in your expectations or overly rigid with your goals, will only interfere with your ability to get things done and make you more stressed and anxious.

An example of Steve's weekly schedule is below. Notice how he used the principles above to create a schedule that is flexible, manageable, and in line with his values:

Steve's Weekly Time-Management Form

Time	Monday	Tuesday	Wednesday	Thursday	Friday	Saturday	Sunday
6:00 am	Wake, shower, shave	Wake, jog	Wake, shower, shave	Wake, jog	Wake, shower, shave		
6:30 am	Breakfast	Shower	Breakfast	Shower	Breakfast		
7:00 am	Drive	Breakfast	Drive	Breakfast	Drive		
7:30 am	Kids to school	Drive	Kids to school	Drive	Kids to school		
8:00 am	Teach	Teach	Teach	Teach	Teach	Wake, jog	
8:30 am	→	→	→	→	→	Shower	Wake, shower
9:00 am						Breakfast	Breakfast
9:30 am						Drive	Drive
10:00 am	→	→	→	→	→	Soccer game!	Grocery shop
10:30 am						→	
11:00 am	Lunch	Lunch	Lunch	Lunch	Lunch		
11:30 am	Teach	Teach	Teach	Teach	Teach	Drive	
12:00 pm	→	→	→	→	→	Out to lunch	Lunch
12:30 pm						→	Call friend
1:00 pm	Plan period	Plan period	Plan period	Plan period	Plan period		

Time	Monday	Tuesday	Wednesday	Thursday	Friday	Saturday	Sunday
1:30 pm	Grade papers	Grade papers	Grade papers	Write rec letter	Syllabi feedback	Drive	Family time
2:00 pm	Teach	Teach	Teach	Teach	Observe class	Clean office	
2:30 pm	→	→	→	→	→		
3:00 pm	Dept mtg		Review syllabi		Detention hall	Watch game	
3:30 pm	→	Drive		Drive			
4:00 pm	Drive	Pick up kids		Pick up kids	Drive		
4:30 pm	Dentist appt	Drive	Drive	Drive	Read, relax?		→
5:00 pm	→	→	Pick up dinner	→	→	→	
5:30 pm	Drive	Kids' homework	Drive	Kids' homework		Drive	Make dinner
6:00 pm	Dinner	Dinner	Dinner	Dinner	Dinner	Pick up dinner	Dinner
6:30 pm	Family time	Family time	Family time	Family time	Family time	Dinner	
7:00 pm	→	→	→	→	→	→	
7:30 pm						Movie night	
8:00 pm	Kids to bed	Kids to bed	Kids to bed	Kids to bed	Kids to bed	→	Kids to bed
8:30 pm						Kids to bed	
9:00 pm							

Time	Monday	Tuesday	Wednesday	Thursday	Friday	Saturday	Sunday
9:30 pm							
10:00 pm	Sleep	Sleep	Sleep	Sleep	Sleep		Sleep
10:30 pm							
11:00 pm						Sleep	
11:30 pm							
12:00 am							
12:30 am							
1:00 am							
1:30 am							
2:00 am							
2:30 am							
3:00 am							
3:30 am							
4:00 am							
4:30 am							
5:00 am							
5:30 am							

You may also notice that Steve didn't manage to fit in every task on his list. Two of his low-priority tasks ("Review AP curriculum," "Revise budget") got bumped to the following week. As deadlines approach, these low-priority tasks may become higher priority and will take precedence over other activities. For now, though, it's fine that they got skipped. Steve felt good about his productivity at work over the week and about the focus he gave to his family and health.

Now you give it a try! Use a copy you've made of the Weekly Time-Management Form to plan your next week. Remember to write in any obligations, appointments, and other necessary activities (like sleeping, eating, and showering) first, as well as the time it takes to get to and from those activities, so you'll know how much time you have to work toward your goals.

Remember to keep your schedule with you so you can refer to it whenever you need to. Try to stick with the plan as closely as possible, but don't be upset if you can't follow it perfectly. Keep practicing and, with each week that passes, you'll gain confidence as you get better at estimating how much time things will take and prove that you can get them done!

SCHEDULING AND TIME-SAVING TIPS

Don't be discouraged if managing your schedule is difficult at first. You may have been procrastinating for a long time—it's a tough habit to break! Keep with it and it *will* get easier. Use the strategies below if you're feeling stuck:

- **Be Flexible**: Don't panic if something comes up unexpectedly. Take a deep breath and give yourself a minute to evaluate whether it's really a high-priority task. If so, bump a medium- or low-priority task to make room. If not, simply plug it in where there's time.

- **Be Realistic**: Remember to be realistic about what you can accomplish. Ask yourself how long things will really take. Be wary of giving yourself far too little or way too much time to complete a task. Both can backfire and lead to procrastination.

- **Forget the Shoulds**: Don't bother with what you *should* do; instead, focus on what you *can* do—leave the impossible expectations behind. So what if your calendar doesn't look like Martha Stewart's? Keep your goals realistic and you will be far more productive.

- **Delegate Whenever It's Appropriate**: Don't be afraid to ask others for help. Be specific in your requests. If you struggle with perfectionism, let go and remember that your way is not the only way to get things done.

- **Remember Your Values**: Prioritize things that are important to you and cross off the things that aren't. It's okay to let some things go. No one can do everything.

- **Use Unexpected Blocks of Time**: If you find yourself with a few extra minutes, use that time to work on something from your list. You don't need to wait until you have the "perfect" block of time to get things accomplished. A few minutes here and there works just as well.

◆ **Don't Be Afraid to Say No**: Turn down requests if you need to and take care of yourself. Don't accept unnecessary responsibilities or projects. You'll be respected more for setting healthy limits than for taking on tasks you can't complete.

◆ **Limit Research**: Set reasonable time limits for yourself on how long you will gather information to make decisions or put together projects. There are infinite resources and limitless data out there. You can't possibly know it all—and you don't need to.

◆ **Use a Buffer**: Leave a few minutes between tasks so you don't rush from one thing to the next. Whenever possible, finish one activity before moving on to the next. Scheduling fewer tasks but finishing them will leave you more relaxed and may actually improve your productivity in the long run.

◆ **If Necessary, Fake It:** Don't wait until you feel like it. Waiting until you're in the perfect frame of mind—with laser focus and no anxiety—will guarantee that nothing ever gets done. Just getting started often leads to feeling focused, rather than the other way around.

◆ **Allow for Realistic Travel Time**: Always plan for the most likely scenario, not the best case. For instance, avoid scheduling only the amount of time that it takes you to get somewhere under ideal weather or traffic conditions.

◆ **Schedule Downtime**: Time to do nothing is critical, and allowing time to recharge your batteries will make you more productive. Scheduling every minute of your day sets you up for failure and will only leave you frazzled and frustrated.

NEXT STEPS

Keep working toward better time management by using this scheduling strategy to plan your weeks. Be sure to stick with it, and give yourself time to improve. If you find that you're still having trouble after a few weeks, review the scheduling tips above and be sure you're using them. If you remain distracted or overwhelmed with the number of tasks on your plate, you may find the upcoming chapters helpful to use in conjunction with your scheduling plan.

Key Points

◆ Better time management is a key step to decreasing anxiety and procrastinating less.

◆ Not just better scheduling, but changing your relationship with time will help you to manage time better.

◆ By developing an awareness of how you spend your time, you can evaluate how closely your time usage matches your values and priorities.

◆ Structuring your day and prioritizing goals will decrease anxiety, avoidance, and procrastination.

11

Change the Way You Relate

Change the way you relate. What does that mean? Change the way you relate to what? Change the way you relate to whom? What *way* do you change? If you're a bit confused by the title of this chapter, take solace. We chose the ambiguous title intentionally. We chose it because, to overcome anxious procrastination, you may need to think about and change the way you relate to lots of things. You may need to change the way you relate to your environment. You may need to change the way you interact with others. And you may need to change the way you view your goals, see your progress, and treat yourself.

Thinking about all of that changing is a little overwhelming, right? It is, if you consider it all at once. But remember, as the Chinese philosopher Lao Tzu put it, *a journey of a thousand miles begins with a single step.* If you follow the steps we outline and make these changes a bit at a time, you'll be surprised at how easily you can improve your relationship with your goals, with others, with your environment, and with yourself.

CHANGE THE WAY YOU RELATE TO YOUR ENVIRONMENT

Some of the biggest hurdles we hear about from our clients in overcoming their procrastination are the temptations and distractions that lure them away from their task—the TV, the phone, the Internet, the refrigerator. It's ironic, because as much as these distractions are inherent to our environment, they are also largely within our control to eliminate (or at least to modify). The phone keeps ringing? Turn it off. The refrigerator beckons? Leave the kitchen. It seems simple, but by making changes to your environment and to the way you relate to it, you can reduce these distractions and improve your focus and productivity.

How Do You Use Your Environment to Procrastinate?

Think for a moment about the ways that you avoid. Everyone is different in how they choose to procrastinate. For some, fear of failure at work may keep them from focusing on a project that is due; instead they choose to vacuum the house, organize the closets, and fold laundry. For someone else, perfectionism may make cleaning the house such an overwhelming task that they prefer to stay at work late, tweaking proposals and calling prospective clients. One person's productivity is another's procrastination (and vice versa). Take a look at the list below and make a checkmark next to the activities that you use to procrastinate.

- ☐ Talk on the phone
- ☐ Watch TV
- ☐ Groom myself
- ☐ Answer e-mail or texts
- ☐ Eat
- ☐ Sleep
- ☐ Exercise
- ☐ Run errands or go shopping
- ☐ Shop online
- ☐ Have sex, masturbate, or watch porn
- ☐ Browse the Internet
- ☐ Clean or organize my desk, car, or house
- ☐ Drink alcohol or do drugs
- ☐ Do more research on the task
- ☐ Pull my hair or pick at my face or skin
- ☐ Read the newspaper, magazines, or books
- ☐ Daydream or "space out"
- ☐ _____
- ☐ _____
- ☐ _____

Notice that we left some lines at the bottom for you to write in any other ways that you procrastinate—remember, the options are different for each individual and are nearly endless.

Now Change It

Now that you have identified the things you generally do to procrastinate, see if you notice any patterns. Do you tend to be pulled away by external temptations, like the TV, the Internet, or other people? Or are you more focused on internal distracters, like hunger, fatigue, or sexual desires? Perhaps you convince yourself that other, less important things need to get done first, like organizing your desk, mopping the floor, or running errands. Pay attention to the things you do most often when you procrastinate, and use the strategies below to begin removing these temptations from your environment.

GET OUT OF THE HOUSE

If you find that when you try to work at home you end up scrubbing the bathtub, alphabetizing your DVDs, or cleaning out your refrigerator, try taking your work someplace else. Being somewhere where you won't be tempted to straighten or organize will allow you to focus on the task at hand. A public library, a quiet coffee shop, or your office at work may just do the trick.

TEMPORARILY BAN TECHNOLOGY

Don't worry—we said *temporarily*! With all the available technologies to stay in touch nowadays, it's a wonder that we're able to stay focused on anything. If you spend too much time checking your Blackberry, consider putting it away for a time. Set a goal to work on your project for fifteen minutes, thirty minutes, one hour—whatever is reasonable—and then turn off your phone and don't check your e-mail or the Internet for that period of time.

HIDE THE DISTRACTIONS

Unplug the TV, or work where you can't see it. Put the newspaper, books, and magazines out of sight. If home is where you need to work, then designate a space there just for working and make it as clutter-free and as distractionless as possible. Take care to not spend too much time setting up this environment—it doesn't have to be perfect, just good enough to get your work done.

STAY AWAY FROM PEOPLE

If you find that being around others gives you an excuse to put your work on hold in lieu of chatting, strategizing, or just plain old people watching, then choose a place to work away from others. If you live alone, perhaps home is the best place. If roommates or family make it difficult, going to the office, finding a secluded spot at the library, or even wearing earplugs may be the solution.

BE NEAR PEOPLE

On the flip side, if you tend to procrastinate by doing things that you wouldn't do in front of others, then find a place to work around people. You'll be less likely to pull your hair, pick at your skin, binge eat, or masturbate in a public place. While you can never entirely remove the distraction of internal sensations like tension, hunger, or sexual desire, being in an environment that is not conducive to acting on these distracters can help you be more productive.

REMEMBER YOUR PRIORITIES

Often procrastinators can convince themselves that other things *need* to be done first, before they can focus on the task at hand. Things like errands, laundry, or returning that phone call take on a sense of urgency that may be misplaced. Before you pick up the dry cleaning instead of finishing your taxes, take a step back to remember your priorities and ask yourself honestly what can wait.

FLIP THE ORDER

Sometimes simply changing the sequence of your activities can make a difference. Of course, we all need to do things for ourselves like sleep, exercise, relax, and have fun. No one can work or be productive all the time. Rather than feeling deprived of things that make a healthy life, be sure to include those things in your schedule—just do some work first. For instance, instead of telling yourself you need to exercise, take a shower, and eat lunch before you can sit down to work on your report, just set a goal of working on it for an hour and then going for a run afterward. You may find that you enjoy that jog even more with some of the weight of work lifted from your mind.

SET A REMINDER

Sometimes procrastination can be accomplished using nothing but our minds. Minutes or hours can pass by while daydreaming, spacing out, or just staring at the wall. If you find that a lot of your time is lost in this way, think of a strategy to bring yourself back to the task. Setting a timer to go off every few minutes or having your screensaver send you a reminder message when you've been inactive too long are just a couple of ideas that may help you break out of that daydream and refocus your mind.

CHANGE THE WAY YOU RELATE TO OTHERS

After you've made some changes in your environment, it's time to take a look at how the way you relate to others may impact your procrastination. As you know by now, there are as many ways to procrastinate and as many reasons for it as there are people who do it. Sometimes putting off a project is really just an indirect way of saying no to something that you never really wanted to do in the first place. Or it could be that trying to do too much actually leads to doing not much at all. Or it could be some of both or something else altogether. We've found that anxious procrastinators frequently take on more responsibility than is reasonable, make commitments to do tasks that are unnecessary, and have great difficulty saying no to others. Whether that stems from perfectionism (*I should be able to do all these things*), a fear of disappointing others (*They'll be upset if I don't help out*), or just a general discomfort with being asssertive (*It's easier to go with the flow*), this way of relating can result in undue stress, worry, and, of course, procrastination. Learning how to assertively decline unwanted obligations and delegate inappropriate jobs can help you focus on the tasks and priorities that really are important to you, reducing your avoidance and procrastination in the process.

What Assertive Communication Is and Isn't

If you often find yourself putting off tasks because you resent having to do them or are frequently angry at yourself for agreeing to do them in the first place, chances are that you're a *passive* communicator. This is actually quite common among anxious procrastinators. Passive communicators prefer to avoid confrontation or disagreement and usually put the needs of others ahead of their own. In doing so, they avoid experiencing arguments or disapproval, but they often feel angry, frustrated, stressed, or resentful as a result. Avoiding or putting off the task provides an indirect means of expressing this frustration and a more comfortable way of saying no.

On the opposite end of the spectrum is *aggressive* communication. Aggressive communicators behave in a rude, demanding way by bowling people over to meet their own needs. People often mistake being assertive with being aggressive. It's a common misunderstanding. In reality, *assertive* communication is quite different from aggressive communication. When we communicate assertively, we strive to meet our needs in an appropriate way while being respectful of others at the same time. The chart below highlights the differences between assertive and aggressive communication.

Communication Styles

Assertive Communication	Aggressive Communication
Respects the feelings of others	Disregards the feelings of others
Enhances relationships	Destroys relationships
Expresses feelings in an appropriate way	Uses maladaptive strategies such as yelling, threatening, or belittling
Fosters respect from others	Leads others to dislike, fear, or avoid you

Remember, assertive communication is focused on appropriately expressing your feelings while simultaneously respecting the rights of others. Learning this effective way of interacting with others will allow you to say no when you want to or need to, so that you won't have to rely on procrastination to "speak up" for you.

How to Communicate Assertively

A client of ours, Jill, was a married mother of three school-aged children who worked full time outside of the home. Jill often put off doing household tasks in favor of other things, like talking on the phone or running errands. As a result, stacks of unfiled papers cluttered her kitchen counters, unpaid bills got lost in the disorganization, and piles of dirty laundry were strewn about the house. After some careful discussion, it became clear that Jill was really resentful that her husband and kids did not help her out more with the housework. A passive communicator, Jill procrastinated about straightening her kitchen and doing the laundry because she was uncomfortable with asking her family to pitch in more and angry that they didn't offer. Avoiding these tasks was her way of indirectly protesting what she felt was an unfair division of labor. Once Jill learned the four key steps to communicating assertively (Bower and Bower 1991), she found that her tendency to procrastinate was greatly reduced. These four steps are:

1. **Defining the situation.** The first step in learning to communicate more assertively is to identify the situation or situations in which you have difficulty being assertive. Try to designate who is involved, when you usually have difficulty, what your usual response is, and what you'd like to be different. For instance, you might find it especially hard to communicate assertively with authority figures, such as a professor or a supervisor. Or you might find situations with a lot of conflict or emotion particularly challenging to your assertiveness skills.

   When Jill defined her situation it looked like this: On the weekends (*when*), my family (*who*) often do their own relaxing things like watching TV or spending time outside, leaving me to do the household chores (*what*). This doesn't seem fair, so I put things off and call a friend or leave to do errands (*usual response*). What I'd really like is for us all to divide up the chores so it's not so overwhelming, get them done, and spend time together as a family (*assertive goal*).

2. **Expressing yourself.** In this step, you express how the situation or the other person's behavior makes you feel. When you discuss your feelings and needs, use *I-statements* to express yourself. I-statements help to get your point across in a way that's not blaming or accusatory. Consider the difference between "I feel upset" and "You make me upset." The first one—with an I-statement— has a much greater chance of success, because it does not blame the other person or lead them to feel defensive.

   So when Jill talks to her family, she could say, "When I'm left to do the household chores on the weekends, I feel it's unfair and I get resentful," or she could say, "You are unfair in leaving me to do all of the chores, and it makes me resentful." Which do you think is a better use of an I-statement? Which do you think is less likely to feel blaming or accusatory to her family?

3. **Proposing a solution.** The next step to assertive communication is to propose a possible solution to the situation. When offering a solution, be sure to be specific and clear, but also be prepared to compromise. Remember, the key to assertive communication is to respect the needs of all parties. Try to state your solution not as a demand but as a firm, clear request. This step for Jill included her presenting the following option to her family: "I've made a list of the usual chores that need to get done every weekend. I would like each of you to choose one chore that you'll do every Saturday morning."

4. **Outlining a consequence.** After proposing a solution, you can outline the consequences of this new arrangement, beginning with the likely positive outcomes. You might describe how this new arrangement will benefit everyone. This is also the time to set limits and discuss any negative consequences if you're unable to reach an agreement or if the other party doesn't follow the terms of the new arrangement.

Jill started by highlighting the positives in her solution: "By dividing up the chores, the house will be neater, I will be less overwhelmed, and we'll have more time to spend doing fun things together." Luckily, Jill's husband and kids were pretty agreeable to helping out, but, had they resisted, she might have moved on to lay out some negative consequences. For instance, with her kids she might have said, "Until your task is completed, you won't be allowed to watch TV or play outdoors." With her husband, a natural consequence may be something like, "If you aren't able to help with the chores and I need to do them myself, then I won't have time to make lunch, so you'll be on your own."

NOW PRACTICE

Remember the steps—define, express, propose, and outline. Think about something that you've been putting off because you feel resentful about it or wish you hadn't agreed to do it, and use the steps to communicate assertively about it.

COMMUNICATE ASSERTIVELY

1. Define the Situation

Who is involved? _____

When does this happen? _____

What usually happens? _____

How do I typically *respond*? _____

What do I want to be *different*? _____

2. Express Yourself

How would you express your feelings in a nonblaming way to the person or persons involved? Using I-statements, write down how you feel about this situation or the person's behavior.

_____

_____

3. Propose a Solution

What would you propose as a solution? Be as specific as possible in your request.

_____

_____

4. Outline the Consequences

What are the positive consequences of this solution?

For you:

_____

For the other person:

_____

What will happen if the situation does not change?

_____

_____

Repeat this exercise in any situation where you find that you take on unreasonable obligations, have a hard time saying no, or agree to do things that lead you to feel resentful.

Troubleshooting

Problems sometimes arise when we try to communicate assertively. Here are some common difficulties and solutions:

◆ Remember that you don't have to respond *immediately*. If you feel pressured or put on the spot, keep in mind that the best strategy is to delay answering until you've had time to collect your thoughts and compose yourself. Don't feel guilty about telling someone that you'll need to get back to them after you've had time to think.

♦ When communicating assertively, you'll inevitably run into someone who behaves aggressively; for example, by responding to your assertion with sarcasm, disdain, or hostility. In these situations, keep in mind that it takes two to argue. Often, the key to disarming a hostile communicator lies in finding common ground. See if you can find a grain of truth in what the other person is saying and acknowledge it. You'll often find the other person softens his aggressive stance, allowing you to move forward toward a solution.

♦ Another common problem is dealing with someone who just won't listen. You attempt to use your assertive communication skills, but the other person just refuses to participate in the discussion. When someone isn't listening to you, it can be helpful to use a technique called *the broken record*. In the broken-record technique you simply repeat and paraphrase your request or response until the person acknowledges it. This technique makes it clear that you won't be swayed and that arguing about it will be ineffective.

♦ Attempting to communicate assertively often involves navigating difficult situations. To effectively use the steps we've outlined, it's crucial to have your own emotions under control. If you're feeling angry or too upset or if the discussion is too heated, try taking a time-out. Taking a step back and allowing everyone to cool off often leads to more productive solutions in the end.

CHANGE THE WAY YOU RELATE TO YOUR GOALS, YOUR PROGRESS, AND YOURSELF

Maybe one of the biggest changes you can make to overcome procrastination is to change the way you think about your goals, the way you assess your progress, and the way you treat yourself. As an anxious procrastinator, you have years of experience in setting unrealistic goals, then focusing on what didn't get accomplished and flogging yourself for it. As a general rule of thumb, overlooking what *did* get done and berating yourself for what did not isn't a very effective motivational strategy. It leaves you feeling discouraged, anxious, and even more likely to procrastinate in the future. Face it—this way of looking at things hasn't really worked out well in the past. Punishment doesn't work all that well in the long term. To really overcome avoidance, you have to suspend this negative judgment and change your focus to what you *are* doing right.

Change the Way You Think About Progress

Anxious procrastinators are quite good at rattling off all of the ways in which they've failed to achieve their goals, while simultaneously discounting any positive progress they've made. How often have you said the following to yourself?

♦ *What I've done doesn't matter because I didn't do* _____.

- *Who cares? It's still not finished.*

- *That was the easy part anyway.*

- *It's only a drop in the bucket.*

- *What difference does it make?*

- *I can't feel good until this is done.*

- *Somebody else would have finished by now.*

How do you feel after reading that list? Revved up and raring to go? Probably not, right? That's because focusing on what you haven't accomplished doesn't serve to get you any more motivated to get things done. It's demoralizing, ruining your self-confidence and sapping your energy. Instead of focusing on what remains undone, try to look at the steps you *have* taken or the progress you've made toward a goal. Change your idea of success from the *outcome* to the *effort*, and you may just find that the outcomes improve too. Try these new thoughts instead:

- *The small steps count too.*

- *I'm closer to my goal than I was before.*

- *Every little bit helps.*

- *I worked hard.*

- *It's better than if I hadn't worked on it.*

- *I'm doing the best I can.*

- *Sometimes things take longer than you expect.*

- *It's about the journey, not the destination.*

Use Positive Reinforcement to Increase Productivity

You need only flip through any introductory psychology book to find out how important positive reinforcement is in changing behavior (Skinner 1965). Positive reinforcement works better than punishment because, if you reward yourself for good behavior, it increases the likelihood that you'll repeat that behavior in the future and make even more progress. Punishment only tells you what *not* to do—it doesn't help you much with how to do better. So, even if you don't accomplish as much as you'd ideally like to or it wasn't perfect, reinforce your efforts. You'll find that it works better than berating yourself or focusing on failures.

IDENTIFY WHAT MOTIVATES YOU

The first step in rewarding yourself is determining what the reward should be. What motivates one person is different than what gets another going, and you may find that which reward works will change depending on the situation. Rewards can be things, experiences, people—it could be anything. So think about what feels good to you. Here are some ideas to get you started:

- Taking a bath

- Getting a massage

- Seeing a movie

- Telling someone about the accomplishment

- Buying clothes

- Listening to music

- Taking a walk

- Buying tickets for a sporting event

- Going out to dinner

- Talking to a friend

- Making a date with your spouse, significant other, or friend

- Taking a bike ride

- Taking time to focus on the accomplishment

- Planning and taking a vacation

- Going to the beach or a park

- Receiving praise from yourself or others

- Reading a book

- Doing nothing

You can use the rewards you thought of in chapter 9 as more inspiration. Consider the whole range of possibilities, including material things, social interactions, leisure activities, or simply the acknowledgement of your accomplishment. Use the spaces below to record your options.

- _____

- _____

- ◆ _____
- ◆ _____
- ◆ _____
- ◆ _____
- ◆ _____
- ◆ _____
- ◆ _____
- ◆ _____

REWARD YOURSELF

Now that you have some ideas about what rewards would be motivating, make sure to reward yourself the next time you make progress toward a goal. This strategy may feel uncomfortable to you, particularly since you may be accustomed to trying to use punishment as motivation. Stick with it, though. Don't worry about being too soft on yourself; remember, the most likely way to increase a behavior in the future is to reward it in the present. Acknowledging success at making an effort will only lead to more effort and more success. Use the following tips to get more comfortable with this new way of viewing your progress and relating to yourself.

Reward yourself. Make sure to acknowledge and reward _any_ steps you take toward your goal. If it's working on your project for fifteen minutes, so be it. You don't have to paint the Sistine Chapel to deserve some accolades, only put in a little effort.

Make rewards commensurate. Try to keep your rewards in line with your effort. If you achieve a big goal, make the reward big. If you take a small step, make it a smaller reward. Remember, though, to consider what an accomplishment is for _you_. Don't base your assessment on what you _should_ have done or how other people would have done it.

Don't delay rewards. Be sure to give yourself the reward as soon after your accomplishment as possible rather than waiting. It's important for your brain to make the link between the behavior and the reward, and this happens more readily when the two happen close together in time.

Don't jump the gun. Don't reward yourself _before_ you've made the progress. As much as it might be tempting to go out to dinner and then start working on your project, for obvious reasons that plan is likely to backfire.

Track your progress. Sometimes simply monitoring your progress can be a reward in and of itself. You may be surprised at how satisfying crossing something off your list can be.

Change the Way You View Tasks

It's no secret that the more people dislike a task, the less motivated they are to complete it. If you see a task as unpleasant or anxiety producing, you're more likely to procrastinate on getting it done (Steel 2007). Focusing only on the unpleasantness of a task can lead to anxiety, distress, and delay. If you find yourself often lamenting how boring or terrible your task at hand is, the following strategies may help.

Use your rewards. Many times, putting forth the effort and completing a task can be the reward in and of itself. However, for those situations that you find particularly aversive, you may find that using the goal-setting skills you've learned may help. Break the dreaded task down into small steps and then use the rewards you listed earlier to give yourself an incentive to complete each step.

Link it to something enjoyable. If you've been putting off something that you find boring or aversive, try to link it to something you find fun. For instance, if you've been putting off looking at a boring prospectus for work, take it outside and sit in the sun while you read. Exercise while watching a television show you like. Mow the lawn with the game on the radio.

Make it social. Turning a task into a social event can be a win-win situation. If you can't bring yourself to study for that biology exam, form a study group. If you're stuck on a writing project, meet a colleague for coffee to go over your discussion points. Clean the attic with a friend. Fusing an aversive task with a social outlet may be just what you need to get over that hump.

Turn it into a game. If you put off tasks because they're too boring, figure out how to make them more challenging. Set a goal for how many calories you can burn on the stationary bike and then beat it. See how many words you can type per minute. Race your roommate to see who can fill a bag with clothes to donate fastest. Find a way to make a boring task more interesting and you will have cracked the code to productivity.

NEXT STEPS

You've taken a look at your environment and made changes to the things that may distract you from making progress. You've practiced communicating assertively with others and saying no to extra responsibilities and obligations. You've learned different ways to approach tasks, think about your progress, and reward yourself for your efforts. If these skills and the others you've learned in this book have decreased your anxiety, worry, and procrastination, congratulations! Now you're ready to move on to the next section, learning how to maintain your progress and continue down the path to productivity. If you're still struggling, look back over the preceding chapters to see if there are exercises you skipped or areas where you may need some continued practice. Good luck!

Key Points

◆ Making changes to your environment can help you overcome anxious procrastination.

◆ Communicating assertively can help you decrease your worry and anxiety and keep you from taking on unnecessary or unwanted obligations.

◆ The four steps to assertive communication are defining the problem, expressing your feelings, proposing a solution, and outlining the consequences.

◆ Thinking about your progress rather than focusing only on the outcome can improve your motivation to complete tasks.

◆ Rewarding your positive efforts will make tasks less aversive and will make it more likely that you will repeat these efforts in the future.

PART 4

Maintain Positive Change

12

Get Support

Overcoming anxious procrastination is often a tough, lonely struggle. Many times, you might feel completely alone and unsupported in your difficulties, like no one understands or could possibly help. Or perhaps you know you need help on a particular task, but you find it hard to ask anyone for assistance, which leaves you stuck in your procrastination and avoidance. Maybe you want someone to offer kind words of encouragement and support as you work hard to make progress on a difficult task. Getting support from others is crucial in defeating anxious procrastination.

This chapter will focus on using your support network to help you in your quest to overcome anxious procrastination and to maintain the gains you've already made. In the coming pages, we'll define social support and describe the different types of support you might need to make your progress permanent. By learning the different kinds of support available to you, you'll be in a better position to access the help most suited to your situation.

SOCIAL SUPPORT

As you continue to work hard to overcome anxious procrastination, it's important to recognize a key asset in your battle: other people. Beating procrastination is a tough struggle, but you don't have to do it alone. Accessing and using your support network can greatly increase your likelihood of success. When you employ others in your fight against anxious procrastination, it means you're using sources of *social support*. Social support is simply someone who provides you with emotional or practical assistance. In this section, you'll learn about the different types of social support, identify your key support people, and learn how to ask for help.

Different Types of Social Support

Social support refers to other people offering you assistance in some way. However, it may surprise you to know that there are different kinds of social support (Cobb 1976; House 1981). Social support can be broken down into four subtypes. These are:

- **Emotional Support.** People who are emotionally supportive are good listeners, make you feel valued, and recognize your strengths.

- **Practical Support.** A person who offers practical support helps you with everyday problems, such as child care, cooking, or finances.

- **Informational Support.** Support here comes from information, guidance, or advice. People who offer informational support may help with important decisions or have special knowledge in a particular area.

- **Peer Support.** This kind of support comes from people who are struggling with procrastination as well or have suffered from it in the past.

For example, Mark was a patient of ours who lost his job about a year ago. He sought therapy because he'd felt anxious and depressed for the preceding six months as dwindling finances forced him to move back in with his parents. One of Mark's main goals was to find a new job. In the beginning, Mark avoided doing the tasks necessary to find new employment. Instead, he'd often sit alone at his computer, surfing the Internet or checking his e-mail, as another day passed without moving forward on his job search.

As Mark worked in therapy, he began to make progress on decreasing his procrastination and started moving forward with actively looking for a job. However, it became clear that Mark lacked the social support that would help him to truly overcome his procrastination and land a job. He would work hard on his job search for a while but then get discouraged and begin to backslide into avoidance and procrastination when things didn't pan out. Once Mark became familiar with the different kinds of support, he decided he needed to access his network to facilitate landing a job as quickly as possible. Mark determined he needed informational support in the form of a career counselor to help him evaluate the job market and create a more effective résumé, emotional support from his friends to help him through this challenging time and keep his motivation high, and practical support from his family, who could help him practice for interviews and find a new interview suit. He also thought that hearing from others who procrastinated would provide him peer support and helpful tips, so he found a discussion board online.

As you become familiar with the kinds of social support available to you, you'll find, like Mark did, that you need different types of support. For example, if you've been putting off completing that presentation for school because your computer isn't working properly and you don't know how to fix it, you need practical support. You'll need to seek out someone—a friend or a computer expert—to help you. Otherwise you'll never complete your project. Likewise, if you're delaying investing in your company's 401k plan because you don't understand how it works, informational support might be necessary for you to move forward toward your goal of saving for the future.

========================

EXERCISE: What Support Do You Need?

Take a moment to identify one task that you're still avoiding and then write it in the space below. Using the list of different types of social support, identify the kind of support that you need to help you complete that task.

Right now, one thing I'm procrastinating on is _____ .

The types of support that I would find most helpful in completing this task are _____

_____ .

========================

Identify Your Key Support People

Now that you're familiar with the different kinds of support, it's time to identify the key players in your support network. Whom can you turn to for the support you need? By recognizing the individuals who make up your support network and the ways they can best help you, you'll map out your social network and quickly know where to turn in times of need.

========================

EXERCISE: Naming Your Social Supports

Who are your support people? Now that you know the different types of support, take a moment to identify the key players for each category in your support network.

Emotional Support:

1. _____

2. _____

3. _____

4. _____

5. _____

Practical Support:

1. _____

2. _____

3. _____

4. _____

5. _____

Informational Support:

1. _____

2. _____

3. _____

4. _____

5. _____

Peer Support:

1. _____

2. _____

3. _____

4. _____

5. _____

As you complete this exercise, it may bring to light some areas where you could use more support. If you had difficulty coming up with resources in each area, you may need to consider ways to bolster your social-support network. Here are some ideas:

- Call old friends you've lost touch with.

- Volunteer in your community.

- Offer your support to a friend or peer.

- Attend social functions at work.

- Sign up for a class.

- Participate in a hobby that involves other people.

- Be friendly and outgoing; seek to constantly expand your social network.

- Ask friends if they know someone who could offer you support in an area you need (for instance, someone who has special knowledge or skills that could be of help to you).

Once you've assessed your social-support network and patched any holes, you're ready to access your network for social support. Here are two additional tips to make the most of your social support:

Communicate assertively. You'll recall from the chapter 11 that to get your needs met, assertive communication is crucial. Assertive communication means communicating in such a manner that you get your needs met while simultaneously respecting the needs of the person with whom you are communicating. Assertive communication is key when you are seeking social support. In order for you to get the support you need to continue overcoming anxious procrastination, you'll need to make assertive requests of other people. Remember, assertive communication has four steps: defining the situation, expressing yourself, proposing a solution, and outlining the consequences.

For instance, Mark used these steps to seek the emotional support he needed from his friends who were well-meaning but sometimes made light of his situation or teased him about living with his parents. As a result, Mark began avoiding interactions with them, but he found this left him even more isolated and depressed. So he first defined the situation (his friends teasing him) and then expressed himself using I-statements by saying, "Whenever you joke about my situation, I end up feeling down and even worse about myself than I already do." He proposed a solution to his friends: "Instead of jokes, what I could really use is to hear any ideas you guys have for improving the situation or maybe just to talk about other things." And then he outlined the positive consequences: "That way, we could hang out more and I'd be less depressed and maybe even get some leads on jobs."

Set external deadlines. Setting external deadlines and having someone to answer to can be an effective motivator for procrastinators and another good way to use your social supports. You saw this strategy in chapter 3 when you made a commitment to change. Publicly stating your goals can make it much more likely you'll adhere to them. In addition, those who know of your goals can check your progress periodically and offer words of support and encouragement. An example of having someone to answer to is an exercise buddy. By publicly committing to exercise and selecting a person from your social-support list to be your exercise buddy, you'll have a partner to monitor your progress, give kind words of encouragement—and push you to get out of bed and hit the gym when you really don't want to go work out. Another example is explicitly stating your work-related goals to a member of your social-support team or even committing to deadlines with them. Again, the hope is that this person will help you move toward your goals by checking in with you and offering you help and encouragement. You can also get support more informally by sharing your goals and plans with several people in your support network.

EXERCISE: State Your Goal

For a task you've been putting off, choose someone from your list of support people and openly state your goal to him or her. Ideally, pick someone whose opinion your care about or whose encouragement you find motivating.

NEXT STEPS

Now that you understand the key role that social support plays in both achieving and maintaining your progress, you're ready to build a firm foundation of support to help you meet your goals. Use the steps you learned in this chapter to access your social-support network, creating a team to help you conquer anxious procrastination. Once your support network is in place, be sure you assess it from time to time to make sure all your needs can be met. Now you're ready for the next step: relapse prevention.

Key Points

◆ Social support—emotional, practical, or informational help from others—is key to overcoming anxious procrastination and maintaining gains.

◆ There are four types of social support: emotional, practical, informational, and peer. By evaluating the type of support you need and who in your support network can provide it, you can get the help you need to defeat anxious procrastination.

◆ Asking for help often requires assertive communication skills. Assertive communication means respecting your needs while also respecting others'.

◆ Setting external deadlines or sharing your goals with others can be an effective motivator in overcoming procrastination.

13

Prevent a Relapse

Overcoming anxious procrastination feels wonderful. After all your hard work battling negative thoughts and avoidance, you can finally watch the storm clouds part and see the sun come out. Productivity and joy return to your life. Your self-esteem increases greatly, and your relationships improve. You feel capable, confident, and in control of your life. It's a feeling you want to last forever.

In this chapter, you'll learn how to use the skills and knowledge you've developed in conquering your anxious procrastination to prevent it from becoming a problem again in the future.

DEFINING A RELAPSE

Once you feel like you've mastered the skills necessary to defeat anxious procrastination, it's tempting to sit back and relax. However, in life there's always another task. There is always another demand that comes your way. So what exactly does it mean to have a relapse when you suffer from anxious procrastination? We use a simple, straightforward definition of relapse in our practice. We believe you've suffered a *relapse* if your anxious procrastination increases again to the point that it significantly *interferes* with your life.

We also believe it's important to set realistic expectations. So let's also talk about what we don't consider a relapse. You haven't relapsed just because you procrastinate at times. It's inevitable that you—like every other human being on this planet—will put off tasks from time to time. It's also a certainty that a task will make you anxious at times and you'll feel a strong urge to avoid it. The good news is that feeling anxious in response to a task at times or putting something off occasionally doesn't mean you've relapsed—it just means you're human.

For example, let's suppose you're a student and you picked up this book because your anxious procrastination caused you to fall behind in your classes. Using the strategies described in this book, you worked hard; over time and with practice, you slowly conquered your anxious procrastination and regained control of your life. You completed all your assignments and finished your classes with satisfactory grades. You feel great and you wonder if you'll ever procrastinate again.

Then you're faced with a difficult project when the next semester rolls around. The professor is requiring a term paper. As you sit down to start working on it, you feel that familiar surge of anxiety and wonder if you'll be able to complete the assignment. You look out your window and see your friends sitting on the lawn, enjoying the sunny day. With nothing done on your paper, you close your books, turn off your laptop, and head outside.

Does this episode of procrastination mean you've relapsed? Fortunately, it doesn't—and it's really nothing to worry about. Remember, in order to meet our criterion for a relapse, your anxious procrastination symptoms have to return at a high enough level to disrupt your life in some significant way.

What are significant ways your symptoms could return to cause a problem? Look back at the problems that drove you to buy this book in the first place. Signs to watch out for include:

◆ Missed deadlines

◆ Incomplete assignments

◆ Complaints from others (friends, family members, professors, supervisors)

◆ Feeling chronically stressed, anxious, or overwhelmed

◆ Frequent fines, late fees, or penalties for avoiding tasks

What is an example of a relapse? Stella is a client of ours who suffered from anxious procrastination while working as a paralegal in a busy law firm. Stella worked hard in therapy and experienced the ups and downs of overcoming a difficult problem. Stella practiced the techniques described in this book and found—through trial and error—the ones that worked for her. Over time, she became more and more skilled at defeating her tendency to procrastinate, and soon enough she no longer considered procrastination a problem.

However, about a year after completing therapy, Stella decided to return to school to become a lawyer. Within the first few months of starting school, Stella's old patterns of procrastination emerged. She found she was falling behind on the demanding reading and assignments required by her professors. As she sat down to work each day, she felt a wave of anxiety—her perfectionist tendencies kicking in—and she would step out for a cup of coffee instead. She received e-mails from her professors about her missing work. First they simply questioned her about the assignments. Then they warned her: if Stella didn't complete her work soon, she'd be kicked out of law school. Clearly, Stella had suffered a relapse.

Entering a challenging new environment had triggered Stella's fears of failure and perfectionism, but fortunately for her, she had all the tools she needed to solve her procrastination problem and succeed in law school. It was just a matter of going back to the strategies that had worked for her in the past. Stella looked at her distorted thoughts that demanded perfect work, used her mindfulness strategies to keep her mind in the present, and kept on track by honing her time-management skills. She worked hard once again and defeated her procrastination once more. Stella completed all her assignments that semester and finished law school on time.

YOUR ANXIOUS-PROCRASTINATION RELAPSE-PREVENTION PLAN

Now that you understand what it means to have a relapse, you're ready to create your personal relapse-prevention plan. There are four keys to this plan:

- Identifying your warning signs

- Knowing what worked for you

- Continuing to practice

- Rewriting your procrastination rule book

Step One: Identify Your Warning Signs

One of the first steps you can take to stop a relapse in its tracks is to know the *warning signs* of a relapse. These warning signs represent the earliest indication that your anxious procrastination is taking hold again, and they appear in different forms. As mentioned above, these may include:

- Feeling anxious, stressed, or overwhelmed much of the time

- Falling behind on tasks or failing to complete tasks

- Complaints from others

This list represents the signs in the order in which they will most likely appear. The first sign is often a general sense of anxiety or stress. You start to feel overwhelmed and under the gun. Your life feels like an endless to-do list, and you just want to shut down and avoid everything. You might be aware of physical symptoms of stress such as an upset stomach or a pounding headache. Or you might notice emotional changes—you're irritable or depressed. Life feels like a constant struggle to keep your head above water.

As a result of these feelings of anxiety and stress you start to procrastinate and avoid—the second warning sign. You favor a nap over that important work project. As you sit down at the computer to work, you surf the Internet instead. You're aware that you're putting off more and more things, and you feel like you're falling farther and farther behind.

Once your anxious procrastination has returned in full force, you'll often become aware of the third warning sign: the unhappiness of others with your avoidance. This could come in many forms. Perhaps your spouse is expressing frustration. Or maybe you just received a poor performance review that cited incomplete assignments. Maybe a client has called to complain about missed deadlines. You might've just found the third notice of an overdue bill in the mail. These are all signs that other people are displeased with your procrastination. Of course, complaints from others are an indication that your procrastination has taken a strong hold of your life again and immediate steps are needed to regain control.

EXERCISE: What Are Your Warning Signs?

Take a moment to identify your warning signs. These warning signs might include anxiety symptoms, signs of interference from procrastination, or problems in your relationships due to incomplete or avoided tasks.

Step Two: Know What Worked for You

Okay, you've identified your warning signs of a relapse. Now take a moment and reflect on the exercises we offered in this book. All of them are effective ways to treat anxious procrastination, but you probably have your favorite techniques, the ones that were the most helpful to you. Maybe labeling distortions in your thoughts held the key to unlocking your anxiety. Perhaps you found mindfulness helped you stay focused, or maybe time management worked well. Probably it was a combination of techniques.

Whatever methods you found useful, those techniques are crucial to preventing a relapse. They are your anti-procrastination tool kit. They are the strategies that you can use time and again.

EXERCISE: What Worked for You?

Use the checklist below to identify the exercises that worked for you. Check off any technique that was helpful, even if it helped only a bit.

- ☐ Labeling distortion in your thinking
- ☐ Generating rational coping responses
- ☐ Examining the root of your fears
- ☐ Practicing mistakes or successes
- ☐ Conducting an experiment
- ☐ Developing better skills
- ☐ Challenging perfectionistic beliefs
- ☐ Banishing shoulds
- ☐ Being average

☐   Tolerating uncertainty

☐   Practicing exposure, either imaginal or in vivo

☐   Developing a mindfulness practice

☐   Examining your values

☐   Setting good goals

☐   Using time-management skills

☐   Making changes to your environment

☐   Communicating assertively

☐   Focusing on progress and rewarding yourself

☐   Using social support

Step Three: Keep Up Your Practice

Defeating anxious procrastination is a true joy. You've worked hard and found great success, and we know how tempting it can be to put all of this behind you, to forget you ever had this problem and move on with your life. No doubt you want to just put this book down and enjoy your newfound productivity and relaxed living.

However, with anxious procrastination, a relapse is often lurking just around the corner. Old habits can be hard to fully put to rest, and it's easy to slide back to your old ways. So to prevent a relapse it's crucial to keep up your practice with the techniques you've learned. Preventing a relapse is kind of like exercise—you wouldn't stop exercising once you've gotten in shape. And we want you to keep working on controlling your procrastination even though you're feeling better.

Of course, after you've overcome anxious procrastination, you might find yourself busier and more productive than ever before. Finding time to practice can be especially difficult. In chapter 10 you learned the importance of scheduling your time. It can be helpful to select a time each week during which you'll practice the techniques that were most effective for you. Of course, you'll be utilizing these techniques in real time as well. However, regular practice outside of daily life can really bolster your skills. You might consider this "therapy time" and plan it just like you would a regular therapy appointment. Take a look back at the exercise "What Worked for You?" above, and, during your therapy time, practice the techniques that you checkmarked. Remember, regular practice goes a long way toward preventing a relapse.

===

EXERCISE: Schedule Practice Time

Use the blank schedule in chapter 10 to fill in specific times each week that you'll practice the techniques that were most helpful to you.

===

Step Four: Rewrite Your Anxious-Procrastination Rule Book

Consciously or not, we all follow our own rule book in life. We have certain guidelines that we follow for living. We often pick these up throughout our formative years, from our parents or important early experiences. Sometimes we don't even realize what our rules are, yet they guide our decisions and behavior every day. As an anxious procrastinator, you have a set of rules that has led you to put things off and avoid tasks. In this book, we've addressed the symptoms of anxious procrastination, its causes, and how to overcome them. Throughout this book, we've shown you specific techniques that address your symptoms and the fears that underlie them, and we've offered you behavioral strategies for change. However, to maintain the progress you've made, you will need to take a look at your rule book and uncover any core beliefs that make you vulnerable to procrastination in the future.

Though these rules lead you to procrastinate and avoid, it's important to remember that these rules usually develop as a *solution*. They solve your feelings of anxiety and fear by encouraging you to avoid certain thoughts or tasks. However, these rules become counterproductive, because by solving one problem, you create another. For instance, let's suppose that you feel intense anxiety every time you sit down to work on a presentation. The deadline is looming, but your anxiety is strong. You feel frustrated, like you have to do it perfectly. The pressure is on. However, instead of working on it, you follow a rule you've developed over time: *When I feel anxious, I should avoid what I fear instead of confronting it.* So you watch TV and surf the Internet instead. By choosing avoidance, you're lessening your anxiety—solving that problem. You're creating another problem, however—the consequences of your unfinished assignment.

To make long-term changes, it's crucial to rewrite your rule book. By changing your rules, you'll make yourself much less vulnerable to having a relapse. Here are some examples.

The Procrastination Rule Book

Old Rules	New Rules
1. Avoidance works: If a situation feels bad, I should avoid it. It's bad to feel bad. Feeling anxious means there's something wrong with me.	1. I can face it: I'll do what I need or want to do regardless of how I feel. Feeling anxious at times is normal and doesn't mean something is wrong with me.
2. Perfection is possible: High standards motivate me. I can't live with mistakes. I won't feel good unless things are "right."	2. Good enough is okay: I realize striving for perfection leaves me paralyzed, so I aim for a standard that allows me to move forward.
3. Failure is unacceptable: I can't tolerate failing. If I'm not sure I can succeed, I shouldn't try. Failing is shameful.	3. Failure is part of life: Everyone has strengths and weaknesses. Failure is a normal part of life. If I'm falling short somewhere, I'll take steps to boost my skills.
4. It should feel right: There is a right time, place, and mood for getting things done. I need to wait for these moments.	4. The time is now. I can accomplish a lot even if I don't feel perfectly focused or motivated. If I have a few minutes, I can get started now rather than wait until later.
5. I shouldn't have to: If something is boring or unpleasant, I shouldn't have to do it. I deserve to have fun.	5. Let's get it over with: Sometimes I need to do things that I don't necessarily want to do. The quicker it gets done, the sooner I can have fun.

NEXT STEPS

Congratulations! You now have all the tools you need to defeat anxious procrastination. Now it's time for you to go out and use your skills to be more productive and less anxious. With less time spent procrastinating and worrying, you'll not only get more done but have more time to enjoy yourself and live life to the fullest. Should you find your symptoms of procrastination creeping back, simply return to the techniques in this book to keep those symptoms in check. We wish you the best of luck and hope you'll find the rewards of your hard work well worth it!

Key Points

◆ A relapse simply means your anxious procrastination symptoms have returned to a level at which they significantly interfere with your life.

◆ Effective relapse prevention consists of four key steps: knowing your warning signs, knowing what worked for you, continuing practice, and rewriting your rule book.

◆ If you suffer a relapse and can't seem to get unstuck, consider seeking professional help from a skilled and caring psychologist or psychiatrist trained in treating problems with anxiety and procrastination.

References

Bandura, A. 1997. *Self-Efficacy: The Exercise of Control.* New York: Freeman.

Beck, A.T., A.J. Rush, B.F. Shaw, and G. Emery. 1979. *Cognitive Therapy of Depression.* New York: Guilford Press.

Bower, S.A. and G.H. Bower. 1991. *Asserting Yourself: A Practical Guide for Positive Change.* 2nd ed. New York: Perseus Books.

Brantley, J. 2007. Calming Your Anxious Mind: How Mindfulness and Compassion Can Free You from Anxiety, Fear, and Panic. Oakland, CA: New Harbinger Publications.

Brownlow, S. and R.D. Reasinger. 2000. Putting off until tomorrow what is better done today: Academic procrastination as a function of motivation toward college work. *Journal of Social Behavior and Personality* 15:15-34.

Burka, J.B. and L.M. Yuen. 2008. *Procrastination: Why You Do It, What to Do About It Now.* Cambridge, MA: Da Capo Press.

Chu, A.H.C. and J.N. Choi. 2005. Rethinking procrastination: Positive effects of "active" procrastination behavior on attitudes and performance. *Journal of Social Psychology* 14:245-264.

Cobb, S. 1976. Social support as a moderator of life stress. *Psychosomatic Medicine* 38:300-314.

Craigie, M.A., C.S. Rees, A. Marsh, and P. Nathan. 2008. Mindfulness-based cognitive therapy for generalized anxiety disorder: A preliminary evaluation. *Behavioural and Cognitive Psychotherapy* 36: 553-568.

Dietz, F., M. Hofer, and S. Fries. 2007. Individual values, learning routines, and academic procrastination. *British Journal of Educational Psychology* 77:893-906.

Effert, B.R. and J.R. Ferrari. 1989. Decisional procrastination: Examining personality correlates. *Journal of Social Behavior and Personality* 4:151-161.

Evans, S., S. Ferrando, M. Findler, C. Stowell, C. Smart, and D. Haglin. 2008. Mindfulness-based cognitive therapy for generalized anxiety disorder. *Journal of Anxiety Disorders* 22:716-721.

Foa, E.B. and M.J. Kozak. 1986. Emotional processing of fear: Exposure to corrective information. *Psychological Bulletin* 99:20-35.

Fritzsche, B.A., B.R. Young, and K.C. Hickson. 2003. Individual differences in academic procrastination tendency and writing success. *Personality and Individual Differences* 35:1549-1557.

Hayes, S. 2005. *Get Out of Your Mind and Into Your Life.* Oakland, CA: New Harbinger.

House, J.S. 1981. *Work Stress and Social Support.* Reading, MA: Addison-Wesley.

Kabat-Zinn, J. 1990. *Full Catastrophe Living.* New York: Delacorte Press.

————. 1994. *Wherever You Go, There You Are.* New York: Hyperion.

Kim, Y.W., S.H. Lee, T.K. Choi, S.Y. Suh, B. Kim, C.M. Kim, S.J. Cho, M.J. Kim, K. Yook, M. Ryu, S.K. Song, and K.H. Yook. 2009. Effectiveness of mindfulness-based cognitive therapy as an adjuvant to pharmacotherapy in patients with panic disorder or generalized anxiety disorder. *Depression and Anxiety* 26:601-606.

Klibert, J.J., J. Langhinrichsen-Rohling, and M. Saito. 2005. Adaptive and maladaptive aspects of self-oriented versus socially prescribed perfectionism. *Journal of College Student Development* 46:141-156.

Ladouceur, R., M.J. Dugas, M.H. Freeston, E. Leger, F. Gagnon, and N. Thibodeau. 2000. Efficacy of a cognitive-behavioral treatment for generalized anxiety disorder: Evaluation in a controlled clinical trial. *Journal of Consulting and Clinical Psychology* 68(6):957-964.

Locke, E. 2002. Setting goals for life and happiness. In *Handbook of Positive Psychology,* eds. C.R. Snyder and S.L. Lopez, 299–312. New York: Oxford University Press.

McCown, W., J. Johnson, and T. Petzel. 1989. Procrastination, a principal components analysis. *Personality and Individual Differences* 10:197-202.

Mehrabian, A. 2000. Beyond IQ: Broad-based measurement of individual success potential or "emotional intelligence." *Genetic, Social, and General Psychology Monographs* 126:133-239.

Milgram, N. and Y. Toubiana. 1999. Academic anxiety, academic procrastination, and parental involvement in students and their parents. *British Journal of Educational Psychology* 69:345-361.

Miller, W. and S. Rollnick. 2002. *Motivational Interviewing: Preparing People for Change,* 2nd ed. New York: Guilford.

Onwuegbuzie, A.J. and K.M.T. Collins. 2001. Writing apprehension and academic procrastination among graduate students. *Perceptual and Motor Skills* 92:560-562.

Senecal, C., K. Lavoie, and R. Koestner. 1997. Trait and situational factors in procrastination: An interactional model. *Journal of Social Behavior and Personality* 12:89-903.

Sirois, F.M., M.L. Melia-Gordon, and T.A. Pychyl. 2003. "I'll look after my health, later": An investigation of procrastination and health. *Personality and Individual Differences* 35:1167-1184.

Skinner, B.F. 1965. *Science and Human Behavior.* New York: Free Press.

Spada, M.M., K. Hiou, and A.V. Nikcevic. 2006. Metacognitions, emotions, and procrastination. *Journal of Cognitive Psychotherapy* 20:319-326.

Steel, P. 2007. The nature of procrastination: A meta-analytic and theoretical review of quintessential self-regulatory failure. *Psychological Bulletin* 133:65-94.

Stöber, J. and J. Joorman. 2001. Worry, procrastination, and perfectionism: Differentiating amount of worry, pathological worry, anxiety, and depression. *Cognitive Therapy and Research* 25:49-60.

Stoeber, J., A.R. Feast, and J.A. Hayward. 2009. Self-oriented and social prescribed perfectionism: Differential relationships with intrinsic and extrinsic motivation and test anxiety. *Personality and Individual Differences* 47:423-428.

Sub, A. and C. Prabha. 2003. Academic performance in relation to perfectionism, test procrastination, and test anxiety of high school children. *Psychological Studies* 48:77-81.

Tan, C.X., R.P. Ang, R.M. Klassen, I.Y.F Wong, W.H. Chong, V.S. Huan, and L.S. Yeo. 2008. Correlates of academic procrastination and students' grade goals. *Current Psychology* 27:135-144.

Van Eerde, W. 2003. Procrastination at work and time management training. *Journal of Psychology* 137(5):421-434.

Wegman, D. 1994. *White Bears and Other Unwanted Thoughts: Suppression, Obsession, and the Psychology of Mental Control.* New York: Guilford Press.

Zinbarg, R.E., M.G. Craske, and D.H. Barlow. 1993. *Mastery of Your Anxiety and Worry: Therapist Guide.* San Antonio, TX: Harcourt Brace.

Pamela S. Wiegartz, Ph.D., is coauthor of *10 Simple Solutions to Worry* and *The Pregnancy and Postpartum Anxiety Workbook*. She is a certified fellow of the Academy of Cognitive Therapy and a member of the scientific advisory board of OCD Chicago. Wiegartz is director of CBT services and training in the department of psychiatry at Brigham and Women's Hospital in Boston and is on the faculty at Harvard Medical School.

Kevin L. Gyoerkoe, Psy.D., is coauthor of *10 Simple Solutions to Worry* and *The Pregnancy and Postpartum Anxiety Workbook*. Gyoerkoe is codirector of the Anxiety and Agoraphobia Treatment Center, a group practice in Chicago and Northbrook, IL. He is certified by the Academy of Cognitive Therapy and serves on the Scientific Advisory Board of OCD Chicago.